# ROCKHOUNDING
# Utah

### THIRD EDITION

## A Guide to the State's Best Rockhounding Sites

## WILLIAM A. KAPPELE

### REVISED BY GARY WARREN

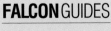

**FALCON**GUIDES

GUILFORD, CONNECTICUT

# FALCONGUIDES®

An imprint of The Rowman & Littlefield Publishing Group, Inc.
4501 Forbes Blvd., Ste. 200
Lanham, MD 20706
www.rowman.com
Falcon and FalconGuides are registered trademarks and Make Adventure Your Story is
a trademark of The Rowman & Littlefield Publishing Group, Inc.

Distributed by NATIONAL BOOK NETWORK

Copyright © 1996 The Rowman & Littlefield Publishing Group, Inc.
A previous edition of this book was published by Falcon Publishing, Inc., in 2014.
This FalconGuide edition 2020

Photos by Gary Warren and his wife, Sally Warren, unless otherwise noted
Maps by Melissa Baker, The Rowman & Littlefield Publishing Group, Inc.

British Library Cataloguing in Publication Information available

**Library of Congress Cataloging-in-Publication Data available**

ISBN 978-1-4930-4596-9 (paperback)
ISBN 978-1-4930-4597-6 (e-book)

∞™ The paper used in this publication meets the minimum requirements of American
National Standard for Information Sciences—Permanence of Paper for Printed Library
Materials, ANSI/NISO Z39.48-1992.

# CONTENTS

## South Utah

## Southeast Utah

# Overview

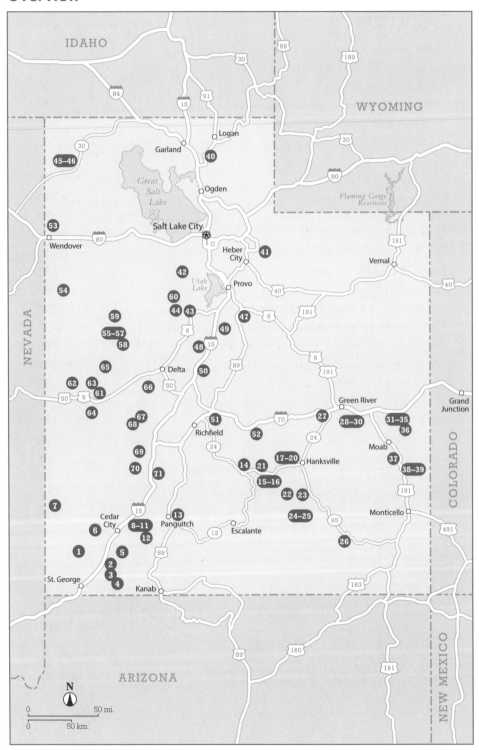

## East Utah

## North Utah

## Central Utah

## West Utah

## Southwest Utah

# ACKNOWLEDGMENTS

I want to start by thanking the many people who contributed to this book and especially to William Kappele, without whose many hours and years of dedication this book would not have been possible. His directions were still good in finding the many sites that are described in this book. I was able to use his directions to take the GPS coordinates that have been added to the book. I want to say a big thank-you to the many friends and members of rock clubs in Utah who answered my many questions. Another big thank-you goes out to David and Kathy Farnsworth, who made the many trips with my wife, Sally, and me to get the GPS readings and to verify that material can still be found at the various sites in this book. They all have a love for the outdoors and enjoy rockhounding almost as much as I do.

Finally, I give my deepest thanks to my wife, Sally, who visited every site in this book with me and kept me on track, writing down the GPS readings and altitudes. Without her help I would have been driving around in the desert wondering where these sites were. She kept me on the right roads and verified mileage and distance. She also made sure I had photos of the various sites we visited and kept track of the log for the photos. We covered more than 4,000 miles researching and revising this book and re-photographing the sites that are featured here.

In 2019 they asked me again to revise and check over what has been in this book. I have added two new sites along with photographs. I have added new information to the Forest Service subsection on page 16 as their rules have changed since this book was revised in 2013, and in the back I have added a new section, "Tools of the Trade," so that you can make sure you have the tools you need with you to go out and find your treasures. I hope that you enjoy this book and use it to help find your treasures in Utah.

Watch for hairpin turns on your way to Boulder, Utah, from Bullfrog Marina.

# ABOUT THIS GUIDE

Anyone who has followed the rockhounding hobby for more than a few years has undoubtedly encountered the two most common types of guidebooks. First is the type that simply lists the material to be found, gives brief directions to the sites, and provides a map that may or may not be accurate.

The second type is more a treasure house of adjectives than a guidebook. Although the material to be found there may look as interesting as a piece of broken sidewalk, it will invariably be described as containing "fiery" reds, "deep, rich" purples, "breathtaking" oranges, and on and on.

Many rockhounds (including yours truly) have driven down miles of dirt roads and hiked over hills and through valleys only to be disappointed because the enthusiasm of the guidebook's author outdid the actual beauty of the find. We will not so mislead you in this book. If we are describing a site where red agate can be found, we will call it simply *red agate*, even if we might think it is "fiery." You will have to be the judge, since beauty certainly is in the eye of the beholder. I have tried to verify all the sites to make sure that material is still available as of 2019, but it is up to you as to whether it is good enough for a cabochon or just a garden rock.

Another problem with some guidebooks is that they list old sites that are no longer productive. Some, in fact, have been rockhounded into oblivion and would not yield enough material for a cabochon if you used heavy equipment. This is not to say that all old sites are not worth visiting, however. Many still provide worthwhile cutting material or mineral samples, but it is not just a matter of leaning out the car window and picking them up. We have listed some of these sites, but we also tell you just how hard and long you may expect to work for your prizes.

All the sites in this book have been carefully checked as to accessibility. For example, we will not send you to a site that is part of a national monument. Grand Staircase–Escalante National Monument falls into this category. When this guide was first published, there were several sites at Grand Staircase–Escalante where rockhounds could explore and collect materials. Under current regulations, you can no longer collect any material from national monuments. I have removed these sites from this edition. We have also been extremely careful to indicate when a site is on private land. Farmers and ranchers are generally willing to let you collect on their property if it will not disrupt their activities, but you must always ask first. Just because there is no posting does not mean that collecting is allowed.

It is also important to understand that all sites, particularly mine sites, are subject to both fluctuations in mineral prices and the whims of their owners. One day a mine may look as though no one had been near it in a hundred years, but within a very short time, it could be reopened and working. If the trip to a listed site is a long one, be sure to check the collecting status locally before starting out. You'll save a lot of time and effort.

There is a lot more to the hobby of rockhounding than simply collecting rocks and hauling them home to fill up your backyard or garage. The facets (no pun intended) of the hobby are many and varied. Some collectors only want to pick up pretty rocks and take them home for displays or for the rock garden. Often these people do not even know the kind of material they are collecting. Many do not care. That's fine.

Some rockhounds are locked into collecting agates and jaspers, walking over a mountain of mineral specimens and not even seeing them in order to get to their favorites. Some collect only what they can use for lapidary; still others want mineral specimens for display or micromounting. There are even those whose interest is in the geology of the area and who don't care if the native rock *does* look like pieces of broken sidewalk.

In short, rockhounds come in a wide variety, and we have tried to offer something of interest to all of them. One word of caution: Some rockhounds are spoiling it for everyone. Most rockhounds use pick and shovel and collect material they can personally use and enjoy. But some try to take everything they can get their hands on and make a profit on the material. They will go into a site and use whatever means necessary, including power and heavy equipment, to fill up a pickup and all their friends' pickups. I have seen places where one year there was material everywhere and the next was completely decimated by indiscriminate rockhounds using heavy equipment. The landowners were threatening to close the whole area, but with some talking they were convinced to leave it open for rockhounds. If you see so-called rockhounds using this method, report them to the authorities. Any state or Bureau of Land Management (BLM) land in Utah does not allow you to use heavy equipment to collect rocks or minerals without a permit. Check the rules and regulations of an area before you go. Most BLM sites and Utah state lands will only let you collect 250 pounds per day, and you can only use hand tools. If you are going rockhounding as a group, check with the BLM; permits are now needed to hunt as a group on public lands. Rock clubs are no exception.

# INTRODUCTION: WELCOME TO UTAH

Perhaps no other state in the Union has more to offer the rockhound than Utah. A true geological wonderland, Utah has an abundance of exposed rock formations that give us a detailed look at the evolution of our Earth. During this evolution, mountains have risen and weathered away, lakes have filled and drained or dried up, and rivers have carved fantastic canyons and gorges. The steep-walled canyons cut by the Escalante and Paria Rivers and the textbook-example goosenecks carved by the San Juan River are only a few examples.

As the seas of the Paleozoic era came and went, varied life-forms evolved. In the beginning, the fascinating little crab-like creatures we call trilobites came on the scene. All these countless millions of years later, we venture out onto the desert and dig for their fossils.

As the Paleozoic era progressed, cephalopods, gastropods, brachiopods and those beautiful horn corals arrived on the scene. Today we search on top of a mountain for the agatized red and black fossils of horn coral. Canyon walls along the Wasatch Range contain fossils of other corals, clams, snails, and sea lilies.

All of this is enclosed in an area of 54.4 million acres, of which 35.5 million are owned by the federal government. More than twenty-two million acres of these federal lands are operated by the BLM. There are five national parks: Zion, Bryce, Capitol Reef, Arches, and Canyonlands. In addition, there are six national monuments: Timpanogos Cave, Cedar Breaks, Hovenweep, Natural Bridges, Grand Staircase–Escalante, and Dinosaur. The USDA Forest Service oversees six national forests: Ashley in the northeast, Dixie in the south, Fishlake in the south-central, Manti–La Sal in the central, Uinta in the north-central, and Wasatch-Cache in the north. There is Golden Spike National Historic Site and Flaming Gorge and Glen Canyon National Recreation Sites. There are also many other state parks and recreation areas throughout Utah. Visit their websites for locations and access to Utah's many natural wonders.

The population of Utah is concentrated along the Wasatch Front. Utah's total population as of July 2019 is 3,221,610, with the Wasatch Front having 76 percent, or 2,448,424 people. Utah's total number of people per square mile is 33.6. Even if this sounds like a lot of people, remember that this leaves only 3.2 people per square mile throughout the rest of the state. This makes for uncrowded rockhounding, but when you are out in the boondocks, you had better take your lunch and have a full tank of gas.

## Topography

Utah is divided into two approximately equal sections by a mountainous spine that stretches from north to south. The northern portion of the spine, the Wasatch Range, runs from the Idaho border to 11,877-foot Mount Nebo near the town of Nephi. From there southward, the spine consists of a series of high plateaus. While the rocky spine divides Utah into two sections, the state actually comprises three rather distinct regions. To the west of the spine, the land is a part of the Great Basin. Over this huge area, rockhounds can find a variety of obsidian, topaz, trilobites, agate, and jasper and mineral specimens around the old mines.

The eastern half of the state is divided into two primary parts. The first is the mountainous region in the northeast where the Uinta Mountains stretch eastward from the Wasatch Range to Dinosaur National Monument on the Colorado border and north to Wyoming. It is in this corner of the state that the black and red horn corals are found. Here too are mineral specimens and some agate and jasper. It is on the Colorado Plateau (which covers the area from the Uintas south to Arizona and from the mountainous central spine east to Colorado) that rockhounding takes on its true meaning. This vast rainbow-hued land of high plateaus and deep canyons reaching to the horizon must have been created with rockhounds in mind. Here you'll find agates and jaspers in myriad colors, petrified wood that rivals the colors of those in Arizona's world-famous Petrified Forest, coprolites (fossilized excrement of dinosaurs), Moqui marbles (strange little sand-filled iron concretions), and a variety of invertebrate fossils.

## A Word about the Weather

Utah is the second-driest state in the Union. Only Nevada can claim less annual precipitation. Just how this will affect you, however, depends on the season and the part of the state where you find yourself. Utah's position on the planet gives it four seasons of approximately equal length. Summer lasts from the end of June until the end of September. Fall runs from the end of September until the end of December. Winter fills the gap until the end of

A rainy day can bring sudden waterfalls in the desert.

March, and spring lasts until the end of June. July's average temperature is 88.9°F; January's low is 12.6°F.

These dates are of course approximate, but they aid in planning trips. In winter, for example, snow covers most of the state at any given time. This too is subject to the whims of Mother Nature. Utah's annual snow fall is 56.7 inches. We have spent Christmas on the Wasatch Front when the weather was more like Southern California than Utah. And we have spent Easter here when it was more like the North Pole. Winter, in general, is not a good time for rockhounding in Utah, but if it is your only chance, make sure you inquire about the weather conditions—and keep your fingers crossed. If you go to the south and west in winter, you might be able to find a piece of agate peeking up through the snow. It will be so cold that it won't be able to run very fast.

Spring is usually a good time for rockhounding, but rain is occasionally a problem. Utah's annual rainfall is 14.7 inches. Sometimes this seems to happen all on the same day if you are out in the desert. Many of the dirt roads can become impassable mud holes, and wandering around in rain and mud takes much of the thrill out of the hunt. Again, check ahead for the weather conditions. It is also a good idea to check locally for flash flood conditions. Remember, the road where you are may be dry and the weather may even be sunny, but between where you are and where you want to be, there may be a washout caused by a flash flood that started high in the mountains far away. We were in Moab one day in 2012 and drove to a site on dry roads, but when we came back the road was covered by a large stream. After four hours we were finally able to get back to dry ground.

Summer is often the only time many of us can get away for a rockhounding trip. Fortunately, all of Utah is good rockhounding country in summer. The southern and far western desert areas can get uncomfortably warm, but they are not like the Mojave. Just observe the precautions listed in the "Have a Safe Trip" section and you will be fine.

Well, if I counted right, this leaves only the fall. In case you haven't guessed by now, fall is my favorite time of year for rockhounding. There are several reasons for this. First, the temperatures are brisk and invigorating. Second, the summer rains have all but gone and the snow has not yet arrived. Third, the fall colors in Utah are spectacular, so you can combine your rockhounding with sightseeing and photography.

Your season may be dictated by vacation time, job demands, and a host of other things. Rest assured, however, that whenever you head for Utah for a rockhounding adventure, you will not be disappointed. All the superlatives fit this beautiful state, so pack the truck, trailer, or car; grab the kids; and load up the bags and hammers. It's time to head for Utah!

# FINDING YOUR WAY

We have made every effort to provide accurate maps with recognizable landmarks and all highway and road designations. The mileages given in the text are as accurate as the odometer on my vehicle. The major problem of course is that, even on freeways, odometer readings will vary; and on jeep roads, where the wheels are constantly bouncing, they are notoriously bad. Thus, the mileage figures must be taken as approximate. Whenever possible, we have included prominent and reasonably permanent landmarks. GPS readings are now included in this guide, but please keep this in mind: When we were doing these readings in 2012, we found that some were off by 20 miles. I took a class on GPS reading and found that to get a reliable reading, you need three points of reference. Some of the canyons we went into and places with thick trees and such made it difficult to get the correct reading. So in verifying the readings, there may be some discrepancies. What I am trying to say here is make sure you know your GPS unit. Take a few readings when you go to these sites to make sure you are close to the correct place. If you are in some of the deep canyons or among trees or anything else that can block readings, move around some and check the map on your GPS unit to make sure you are getting signals from at least three different satellites. All GPS readings in this book are or should be accurate to within a few meters.

Standard highway maps help in getting you to the point where our maps start. US Geological Survey (USGS) topographic maps are indispensable for hikers, but for our purposes they are not very helpful; they do not usually show most of the kinds of roads we use, and the ones they do show are often very inaccurate. We have used one of the new maps from *Utah Road and Recreation Atlas*, put out by Benchmark Maps, and have found it to be very accurate. This can be used with a small graph that will give you GPS coordinates for all of Utah. If you are going to purchase one, get the edition with the black bar instead of the red bar on the top of the book. This edition has GPS grids, and you should be able to find all the sites in this guide by using the GPS readings in this book and the atlas as a reference.

Most old dirt roads and tracks were built to get to a specific destination that has long since been abandoned. These roads may have deteriorated from lack of maintenance, but they generally still go to the original destination. In some other areas, however, there may be a new fork here and there that didn't exist when the map was drawn. Usually these new roads are readily identifiable as new, but once in a while a little backtracking is necessary. It is part of the fun, and you just might make a new discovery.

We have indicated the type of vehicle necessary to get to all the sites described in this guide. On some roads the family sedan is fine, but much of the time a pickup or other high-clearance vehicle is needed. For some spots a four-wheel-drive vehicle is absolutely necessary. We used my Yamaha Rhino to travel most of the roads and back trails and were able to get to most of the sites that required a hike when the first edition of this book was published. Remember too that the time of year you visit and the length of time since the road was maintained can change a road from one suitable for the family car to one requiring four-wheel drive. Make sure you have the right type of vehicle before you start. If you have any doubts, make local inquiry about road conditions before you head out.

# HAVE A SAFE TRIP

The rockhounding sites in this book are located both in the mountains and in the desert. It is important for anyone venturing into these areas to be aware of the special rules of safety for each region. I assume that all rockhounds know the simple rules of outdoor safety, so no attempt will be made to lecture on such things as wearing goggles and hats and using sunscreen.

A few unique precautions must be taken in the mountains and in the desert and can mean the difference between an enjoyable trip and a miserable one. In some cases failure to follow the proper precautions can even mean the difference between life and death. If you are an experienced mountain and desert driver and rockhound, you can skip this section. But if you are new to these areas, take a minute to absorb the information in our discussion of things to watch out for. You may avoid a ruined trip or serious injury.

This chapter is divided into four general categories: mountain safety, desert safety, driving safety, and weather safety. Often the four are interrelated.

## Mountain Safety

Just the word *mountain* brings to mind cliffs, peaks, drop-offs, and generally dangerous places. These can all be true, but danger need not be a part of it if some simple precautions are taken. First, be sure you are in shape for the altitude at the site you will be visiting. If you live at or near sea level and go up to 1,000 feet to 10,000 feet or more (which is about all of Utah), be sure your brain tells your body what it is in for. Hiking, climbing, and scrambling up and down tailing piles or quarry walls can put a severe strain on your cardiovascular system, so proceed with caution!

If you experience nausea or shortness of breath (warning signs of altitude sickness), get to a lower altitude as soon as possible.

If you are in a particularly rough or remote area, plan to be out by dark or carry camping gear and food and water with you. Remember, if the road looked rough or had some steep drop-offs on the way in, think what it would be like in the dark.

Many old quarries are flooded. Be extremely careful around them. It is difficult to tell how deep the water is, and the walls are often too steep to climb should you fall in.

Tailing piles around old mines are often very slippery and unstable. You could slide a long way. Even if you take such a slide and aren't hurt, think about the climb back up.

Finally, although it seems obvious, wear proper footwear. In the mountains you will be walking over lots of rocks (and not the kind you want to pick up and take home), and it is easy to sprain an ankle.

## Desert Safety

Probably the most important safety rule for the desert explorer is to travel in pairs or groups. If you have to go alone, let someone know your destination and expected time of return. Only the most dyed-in-the-wool (crazy) rockhounds venture into the desert in the summer months. If you are one of those, be sure you leave your will or living trust with a responsible individual. Desert areas in Utah can reach into 100°F-plus during summer.

Even in winter the desert can be an unforgiving place. Be sure you have plenty of water and an emergency supply of canned or dried food. Canned is better because it contains water; dried food just uses up your precious water supply.

Beware of critters. Because of the daytime heat, most desert-dwelling critters are nocturnal. Since you probably won't be rockhounding at night, you may never see some of them. Snakes are a big worry to many people, but most snakes have a rather narrow band of temperature in which they can function. Too hot and they are dead; too cold and they are immobile. Somewhere in between and they can get you.

Here are some myths about rattlers: The first is that old picture of a rattlesnake sunning itself on a hot rock. In the heat of a desert day, if you see a rattler on a hot rock, it is either a belt or a hatband. Second, unlike the snakes in those sci-fi movies, snakes do not follow people and attack them. That doesn't give the snake much credit. If you saw something about a bazillion times bigger than yourself, would you run up to it and punch it? What would a snake do with you? It can't eat you. It can't make a belt or a hatband out of you. Besides, it's afraid of you.

Now this in no way means you should just assume you can forget about snakes. You absolutely cannot. Snakes do not like the direct heat of the sun, so in the daytime they are usually in holes in the ground, under logs, in rock piles, or hiding in other like places. The best advice is not to put your hands or feet where you cannot see them. We have been at many diggings where we found snakes under rocks or sagebrush. In one area where we were rock-hounding in 2012, we found about thirty snakes in one pit under rocks. I say about thirty. I don't really know, because after I counted four, I was headed down the hill. The people with me told me afterward, when they found me about a mile away.

Scorpions can be nasty critters too. They also are nocturnal, so use the same precautions as with snakes. We had stopped at one pit just at dark and pulled out our sleeping bags to get some sleep. After we were settled down, I looked around and saw a scorpion walking between the sleeping bags. If you have to sleep in the desert, try to get up off the ground if possible. It may save you from waking up to a nasty bed companion. Following this advice will make it possible to have a very safe desert trip. In fact, you may go for years and seldom if ever encounter a snake or scorpion.

There are some man-made hazards in the desert too. Old mines are always dangerous, but the desert mines are especially so. Unlike the hard-rock mines in the mountains, desert mines are often dug in sand and shored up with timbers. As the timbers rot away with time, the mine becomes a big hollow bubble under the ground. Cave-ins are common where the miners dug too close to the surface. Don't ever go into an old mine, and be extremely careful when walking around desert mines. There are often unmarked shafts, and there is the ever-present danger of a cave-in. Remember that snakes and scorpions like cool, dark places during the day, and most mines provide the perfect environment.

## Driving Safety in the Mountains

Many, if not most, of the old mine and jeep roads will be one lane with only occasional pullouts for passing. If you drive roads like this for long, sooner or later you will meet another vehicle going the opposite direction and there will be no pullout. This is one of those situations we all dread, but they happen, and it is important to know just how to handle them when they do.

Remember the most important rule: **The vehicle traveling uphill has the right of way.** The reason is that it is much more dangerous to back down a hill than up one; it is easy for a vehicle backing down to get going too fast and get out of control.

While you want to do everything you can to avoid confronting another vehicle head on, it will probably happen. In order to make the situation as panic-free as possible, keep a few things in mind as you drive. First, try to remember where the turnouts are. Knowing where the closest turnout is will help your peace of mind if you have to back up to one. Second, keep an eye out for approaching vehicles as far ahead as you can. Even though you may be going uphill, if you see a vehicle coming and can pull over near where you are, do so and prevent a potential conflict. Unfortunately, not all drivers offer this courtesy; some will just keep coming as though the road will suddenly widen out.

Finally, don't panic; and don't try to pass the other vehicle or let it pass you unless you are 100 percent certain that it is safe to do so. I have seen vehicles try to pass by driving onto the uphill bank and tipping dangerously. I have also seen them go perilously close to the drop-off. Just stay calm, and, if you are the vehicle going downhill, back up slowly and carefully. The rocks will wait.

It is certainly not a crime to be a novice when it comes to back road and mountain driving, but it may well be a crime not to admit it. There will be times when you crest a hill and see only sky in front of you. The road drops down, but you cannot see it over the hood. The novice who thinks he or she is a pro will drive on, betting that the road goes straight ahead and doesn't take a sharp turn. The sensible driver will stop and have a passenger get out and take a look or will stop the engine, block a wheel with a convenient rock, and take a look. Doing this may seem "sissy" or too time-consuming, but it can prevent an accident or even death.

A similar situation concerns shelf roads and other roads that would be difficult to back out of. I know of a few shelf roads in Utah. The road looks all right as it begins, but it rounds a blind curve and ends at a washout. It is barely one lane, and the drop-off is hundreds of feet. Backing out of a situation like this is not enjoyable. If you find yourself on a road where you are not sure of being able to turn around, get out and walk a ways. It will save you time, potential embarrassment, and possible serious injury. The bottom line: If you aren't sure of the road condition, find out. If you can't find out, don't go.

## Driving Safety in Deserts

In desert driving safety, as in general desert safety, the primary rule is: Don't go alone if you can help it. If you must go alone, be sure that someone knows where you are going and your estimated time of return.

The big culprit in desert driving is sand. First, be sure you have a vehicle that can handle sandy roads. We will tell you the conditions at each site at the time of our visit, but conditions can change, so you should always be on the lookout for problem areas. If you do much desert driving, sooner or later you will get stuck in sand. Even the best of the four-wheel drives can end up in this unhappy situation, so don't buy a disguise and change your name if it happens to you. Be prepared, know what to do, and you will come out of it intact.

Be sure to have a good shovel with you. A full-size model is best, but if space is a problem, one of those folding shovels will do. A tow strap is a good idea too. If there is another vehicle in the party, you may get pulled out.

If you have the space in your vehicle, a little pile of old boards can be a lifesaver. Another nice accessory is a small air compressor. You can do without it, but if you have room, take one. I take my large air compressor in the back of my truck and have had many occasions to use it. Just about any time we go out to the Dugway geode beds, there is someone there with a flat tire or low tire that needs help. From the Dugway geode beds, it is 50 miles just to a paved road and then more miles to a service station to get a tire fixed.

Another thing I have found helpful is a can of tire sealer. I have used this in my Rhino tires a few times, and it has saved me a walk back to camp. I have also used this to help people fix flats at the geode beds and other places. Finally, have a good jack. This will probably not be the one that the factory put in your vehicle. The best way to find a good jack is to talk to the folks at a local off-road store. Different types of jacks work better with certain vehicles, so talk to the experts before you buy.

The best way to avoid getting stuck is to know what you are driving on. If the stretch ahead looks sandy or suspicious, get out and walk it. It may be macho to plow ahead, but macho can cost you a lot of time and labor. If you find yourself in soft sand, keep going. If you stop, chances are you will not be able to get started again and will just dig a hole.

When your forward progress stops, get off the gas pedal and put the transmission in neutral. Climb out and assess the situation. Your first decision will be to determine which way to go. If you just entered the sandy area and the road ahead looks bad, you may want to back out. On the other hand, the situation may be just the reverse. When you have decided which way to go, get out your shovel and start moving sand away from the wheels in the direction you want to go. If you brought boards along, put them ahead of the wheels.

Get back in the vehicle and *ease* it forward (or backward). If you get going, try to *keep* going. Keep a soft foot on the throttle. If you give it too much gas, you will just dig another hole.

If you can't get your vehicle moving, try jacking the wheels up one at a time and put your boards or some branches, rocks, anything you can find, under the wheels. This may get you going. If nothing else works, try letting about half the air out of the tires. This will make a broader footprint and may allow you to "float" over the top of the sand. Be careful of gullies and washes. Where there was a road yesterday, there could now be a deep gully. This is especially true if you are in the southeastern part of the state, where rain showers are frequent and where small dry streambeds can become gullies in a matter of a few hours.

## Weather Safety in the Mountains

Weather can change rapidly in the high country, and you must be ready for it. If you are heading into the 11,000- to 12,000-foot levels, be ready for rain, hail, or snow—even in July and August. Be sure you have both rain gear and warm clothing along. Have some sunscreen too. The sunlight isn't filtered as much at 12,000 feet as it is at sea level, and even though the sun may not feel hot, it will fry your bald spot or blister your nose before you know it.

The weather can be a real problem for driving anywhere, but on a remote jeep road, it can be much worse. Note the road surface as you go along. A road that looks like friendly dirt can become so slick in the rain that you might rather have ice. Old mine roads are given minimal maintenance at best, and a rain that doesn't look too bad can cause washouts that will be impassable. If you are up in a remote area and rain is impending, think about the road you drove to get there. Maybe you should pack up and leave. There is always another day to hunt, and it might be a long walk if the road washes out.

Don't let these gloomy prospects deter you from the fun of rockhounding in the mountains, but do practice good old horse sense. It will make your experience one to look back on with pleasure.

## Weather Safety in Deserts

When most people think of desert weather, they think of hot summer sun and maybe some wind. These happen of course, but so do rainstorms and flash floods. In Utah many rockhound sites are in desert areas but close to the mountains. The most fearsome thing to have happen is to see a wall of muddy water come crashing down a "dry" wash in the middle of a bright sunny day. The rain was miles away in the mountains, but the water ended up in the washes way out on the desert. If you were unfortunate enough to be in such a wash at the time of a flash flood, you would be lucky to survive.

*Never* camp in a wash. These wide washes may look like great camping spots, and may provide some shade and shelter from the wind, but they can become raging rivers within a moment's notice. This is also something to think about when driving. Do you have an alternate route out in case a wash floods? The nice part of all this is that, in many cases, in an hour or so the wash will be dried up and look as though there had been no water in it in a hundred years.

As with the mountains, a little horse sense goes a long way in tackling desert weather. Wear a hat and sunglasses, use sunscreen, and wear loose-fitting clothes and shirts with long sleeves.

## Abandoned Mine Safety

The dangers surrounding abandoned mines would appear to be apparent, but many people just seem to forget. They forget, for example, that falling down some of the deep shafts would be similar to falling off a tall building. Because the distance is not readily visible, the danger is masked. All shafts, portals, and drifts should be avoided. Many of the old mines have been left to the elements for nearly a hundred years, and the shoring has probably rotted away. It is also good to remember that the engineering in many of the mines was often hit or miss to begin with, so many of the mines may not have been safe when they were originally opened up. The best advice is to never enter an abandoned mine. Decayed timbers and open shafts are only two of the many hazards.

Many of the old mines are wet, and pools can sometimes be deceptively deep. It is not unheard of for someone to drown in a mine. Bad air is another possibility. Nothing the mountain may have to offer is worth suffocating to get. One thought should keep any sane person out of such danger: If there were riches worth risking life or limb for down in the depths, then why was the place abandoned? Utah BLM is now putting in bars and locking up entrances to mines no longer in use. You can no longer take anything from mines that have been locked.

Children must be watched constantly. Of course they have to be kept away from the underground workings, but there are many more kinds of trouble they can get into. Many of the sites listed in the book, and virtually all the mines, are on very steep mountainsides. In addition, the tailings piles are steep and often unstable. While it might not be fatal, a slide down a large pile could result in broken bones and other serious injuries a long way from medical help.

These cautions are not meant to keep the reader from exploring these fascinating spots for fear of some waiting disaster. There is no reason such exploration cannot be safe and pleasurable. A good dose of caution and common sense can ensure that it will be.

Happy hunting!

# ROCKHOUND ETIQUETTE

All land belongs to somebody. Those of us who live in a city have no trouble with this concept when we are in our own areas; we don't question the fact that even the rare vacant lot is not available for public use. But when we get out into the wide open spaces, we sometimes forget that just because there is nothing on the land and there are no KEEP OUT signs, permission to enter is not given automatically. Every square inch of the United States belongs to somebody.

Utah, for example, covers approximately 54,300,000 acres. Of these, about thirteen million acres are privately owned. The rest is owned either by the federal, state, or local government, with a small amount given over to Indian reservation lands. Each private owner makes his or her own rules for rock collecting, and each governmental agency does the same. If we are to be responsible rockhounds and keep the lands available to us, we need to know and follow the rules and regulations.

## Unwritten Rules

It is sometimes hard to remember, especially when hunting around some of the old mining areas, that we should try as much as humanly possible to leave the land looking as though we had not been there.

If you do a lot of digging, fill in the holes before you leave. Don't dismantle old buildings, even if you want to make picture frames or a coffee table with that beautiful weathered wood. Always leave gates as you find them. If the gate was closed, close it behind you. If it was open, even though it may seem wrong, leave it open.

It should go without saying that you carry out any trash you brought in, and it won't hurt if you take out any that someone else may have left. The cleaner we keep these sites, the better the chances they will stay open.

## Bureau of Land Management

The BLM defines a rockhound as one who collects rocks, minerals, and fossils as a hobby. Therefore, rockhounding is permitted on all BLM lands with a few restrictions.

First, the rockhound must not create a significant disturbance. This is a little vague, but common sense tells us that we should not dig to the point where we cause erosion of the land or pollution of streams or other water sources. Nor should we drive our vehicles on soft soil where the wheel tracks will create gullies and promote erosion.

Small amounts of rock and mineral specimens are allowed to be collected, but "small" is not really designated. The rules are to differentiate between recreational collectors and commercial miners, so it seems that if you can lift your rock bag and carry it to your vehicle, you are probably okay. There are more-specific rules for petrified wood. Twenty-five pounds per day per person, not to exceed 250 pounds per year, is the limit. Again I bring up the so-called rock hunter who wants to fill up his truck and those of all his friends. If you see someone like this, report him. It may keep us all out rock hunting instead of getting everything shut down. Fossil collecting also has some special regulations. Plant and invertebrate fossils may be collected except in designated areas. Vertebrate fossils, fish, mammals, etc., may not be collected on BLM lands.

If you want the latest information on the collecting status of various areas or want some directions, maps, etc., drop into the local BLM office. Check the local phone book or call or write the BLM main office in Salt Lake City.

## USDA Forest Service

Since I first revised this book, the Forest Service regulations have changed. The Forest Service rules and regulations are essentially the same as those of the BLM. The Forest Service does not have the 25-pound or 250-pound limit on petrified wood but specifies small quantities. On April 17, 2015, the Forest Service enacted a law where you can no longer actively collect fossils on Forest Service land. If you are walking down a trail and see a fossil laying on the ground, you can pick it up but you cannot use a hammer or any other form of tool to take the fossil. I have just made it a practice to not hunt on Forest Service land. Check your local offices of regulations before you go walking and hunting rocks on Forest Service land.

## State Lands

Collecting is not permitted in state parks but is permitted on other state lands, subject to a nominal annual fee and permit. The permit is for an individual or family and allows collecting of 25 pounds plus one piece per day to an annual amount of 250 pounds. For further information contact:

Utah Division of State Lands and Forestry
355 West North Temple
3 Triad Center, Suite 400
Salt Lake City, UT 84180-1204

## Private Property

I cannot overemphasize the importance of getting permission before collecting on private property. Owners of farms and ranches are usually very good about allowing those who ask to collect on their property if it will not interfere with their operations. The only real problem is with some of the land in the wide open spaces, where there are often no houses around or anyone to ask permission of for many, many miles. The only way to gain access to such spots is to go to the county recorder's office and try to find a name and address for the owner. This is a time-consuming process, but if the site looks particularly good, it might be worth the effort. Please, though, resist the urge to enter the land just because there is no one watching.

In the case of mines on public lands, it is reasonable to assume that if there is no posting and no signs of recent work, it is probably okay to collect. There is a small group of "miners" who feel that putting a sign of any kind on a rock site guarantees them access to half the western United States. If you think that this is the case, check it out at the local forest service or BLM office.

## Where Collecting Is Prohibited

Collecting is not allowed in national parks, state parks, or national monuments. The best rule of thumb for determining collecting status is to ask the owner—whether that is a private land owner or a government agency.

# SIGHTS ALONG THE WAY

## Arches National Park

In the red-rock country of the southeastern part of the state, an amazing conglomeration of tall sandstone spires, balanced rocks, and natural arches lures travelers to Arches National Park. The area is composed of deep canyons and gorges, slickrock, and the beautiful sandstone arches from which the park takes its name. Many of the canyons and gorges have sweet-water springs in them, which probably explains why the area was first discovered by cattlemen looking for places to graze their cattle in this otherwise arid land.

It is doubtful that either the cattle or the cattlemen were concentrating on the beauty of the arches, which range from a few feet across to monsters that would allow a small army to march through. There were those far-sighted pioneers, however, who did see beyond just the grazing of cattle. Among them was Alexander Ringhoffer, a prospector who talked Frank Wadleigh, an official of the Denver and Rio Grande Railway, into visiting the area.

Evidently, Wadleigh was impressed—he recommended that the National Park Service designate the area a national monument. The NPS agreed, and in 1929 President Herbert Hoover proclaimed the 4,520 acres of Arches a national monument. Over the years the monument was expanded and improved, until in 1971 it was declared a national park, with an area of more than 70,000 acres.

If you are anywhere near the area, you owe it to yourself to visit this geological wonderland. Take plenty of film or memory cards.

**Finding the site:** From the town of Moab, drive north for 5 miles on US 191 to the turnoff to the park entrance and visitor center.

**For more information:** Arches National Park, PO Box 907, Moab, UT 84532; (801) 259-8161

## Bingham Canyon Copper Mine

Southwest of Salt Lake City, in Bingham Canyon in the Oquirrh Mountains, lies the world's largest open-pit copper mine. First discovered in 1863, the mine was worked mostly for gold, silver, and lead until 1906, when the operations began to concentrate on copper.

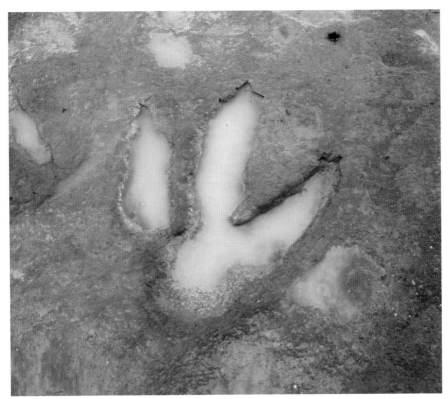

In Moab others have traveled here before you. Don't just look for rocks.

The pit is an amazing sight to see, but the statistics are almost as amazing. Since the mining began, the pit has been excavated to the point where it is now 2.5 miles in diameter and 0.5 mile deep. This hole is the result of the removal of more than five billion tons of rock. (How many rockhounds' rock bags would it take to achieve such a feat?) From that impressive pile of rock, twelve million tons of copper, with significant amounts of gold, silver, and molybdenum, have been extracted.

**Finding the site:** If you are in the Salt Lake City area and would like to visit the mine, take I-15 to exit 301 at Midvale. From here, take UT 48 through Copperton to the mine. There is a fee per car to enter. You really should see the huge open pit before you leave Utah.

**For more information:** Call (801) 322-7300 to hear a recording about the mine tour before you go.

## Bryce Canyon National Park

To many people throughout the country, the names Bryce and Zion are synonymous with Utah. Though different in their geology, they are among the major natural wonders of the world. Bryce Canyon is an absolute wonderland of strange and beautiful geological formations. Evidently, the beauty of the canyon eluded Ebenezer Bryce, an early Mormon pioneer for whom the park is named.

His often-quoted description of the area: "Well, it's a hell of a place to lose a cow."

Though he may or may not have appreciated the beauty of Bryce Canyon, a later settler, Reuben Syrett, whose nickname was Ruby, did see the commercial potential. In 1924 he built the now famous Ruby's Inn. No doubt his business profited greatly from the tours organized by the Union Pacific Railroad in the 1920s. These tours and their advertising helped make the name of this remote canyon in a far-off state known throughout the United States.

When you visit the canyon, you have a variety of options on just what and how much you see. You can drive the scenic loop, stop at the various lookout points, and take great pictures of the formations. If you are more energetic and/or have more time, you can don your pack, hike into the canyon, and get up close and personal with the geology. However you choose to see it, you must not miss this site when you are in the state.

**Finding the site:** If you visit Casto Canyon, drive south for 2.5 miles to the intersection of US 89 and UT 12. Go east on UT 12 to the intersection of UT 63. Take UT 63 right to the park entrance.

**For more information:** Bryce Canyon National Park, Bryce Canyon, UT 84717; (801) 834-5322

## Canyonlands National Park

Canyonlands is a very different kind of national park. While Bryce and Zion can be visited in your Ferrari on civilized paved roads, most of Canyonlands is very primitive. Covering more than 527 square miles and split by the Green and Colorado Rivers, this huge area is served by only a few short paved roads. It is possible to get a bit of the feeling of the area from the pavement, but four-wheel drive and good old-fashioned hiking are the only ways to really begin to understand the character of this magnificent place. There are many hiking trails, but there are also vast areas where there is no sign of people having been there. This unique park is actually four parks in one. They have no roads connecting them, so visitors will have to leave one and drive to the entrance of another. Each district has its own visitor center.

The **Island in the Sky District** has paved roads along the upper rim, which offer grand vistas of the area at numerous overlooks. There are also short hiking trails to many of the more prominent features, such as Whale Rock, Aztec Butte, Mesa Arch, and Upheaval Dome.

The **River District** is noted for the river-running trips through the canyons of the Green and Colorado Rivers. Trips vary from rather leisurely floats to the wild ride through Cataract Canyon down 14 miles of rapids to Lake Powell. Permits are required for these trips, and proper equipment and knowledge of the art of river running are essential.

The **Maze District** is the most primitive of the districts. It was not until the uranium boom of the 1950s that any roads at all penetrated this rugged terrain. If you have any aspirations of exploring the Maze, have a rugged four-wheel-drive vehicle, sturdy hiking boots, or a horse. It will be hard work, but the adventure of a lifetime.

The **Needles District** is noted for its beautiful rock formations. Spires, monoliths, and arches can be seen in almost any direction. You can take advantage of a paved road, several four-wheel-drive roads, and many hiking trails to get a closer view of them.

**Finding the site:** Because of the size of the park and the unique four-district setup, it may be best to go to the information center in Moab at the corner of Main and Center Streets to get directions to the area you want to visit. Alternatively, you can write or call park headquarters.

**For more information:** Canyonlands National Park, 2282 Southwest Resource Blvd., Moab, UT 84532; (801) 259-7164

## Capitol Reef National Park

Far more civilized than Canyonlands, Capitol Reef National Park can be enjoyed by car from paved roads. Of course, if you want to see it all up close, you will have to drive on some dirt and/or do a little hiking.

Capitol Reef got its name from the huge, convoluted upheaval of Waterpocket Fold. To the early settlers, this tall red wall looked like a reef in the ocean. The surrounding domed red hills reminded them of the capitol dome in Washington, DC. I guess if any of us were out here in the heat of summer with nothing to do but chase an occasional cow, we might see a lot of things in the rock formations.

In fact, there are a lot of things to see in these formations. Although typical of the formations throughout the Four Corners region, the ones at Capitol Reef are especially nice. When the gigantic forces within the Earth began their upheaval and squeezed the sides of Waterpocket Fold high into the air and sculpted the surrounding landscape, they left a landscape of strange beauty. If you are visiting rockhounding sites near Hanksville or Torrey, be sure to do a little exploring in this unique area.

**Finding the site:** From Torrey, drive 11 miles east to the turnoff to the visitor center at the park.

**For more information:** Capitol Reef National Park, Torrey, UT 84775; (801) 425-3791

## Cedar Breaks National Monument

If you visit the sites in and around Cedar City, you will have a hard time not seeing Cedar Breaks. The paved road that runs past these sites also passes the major overlooks to the marvelous erosion that is the monument. The giant amphitheater, more than 3 miles across and 2,500 feet deep, is filled with formations much like those at Bryce Canyon. The normally white limestone on the walls and in the formations has been stained with a number of minerals to provide a rainbow of warm earth colors.

In fall the colors of the leaves in the canyon are breathtaking; in the spring more than 150 species of wildflowers cover the high meadows. At an altitude of well over 10,000 feet, the growing season is short, though. If you want to see the wildflowers, the end of July is usually the best time. (In the mountains of Utah, spring comes roughly in July due to the high altitude.) This varies with the length and severity of the winter, however. I have been to this spot when there was still snow on the ground at the end of July. If you are traveling a long way, it would be a good idea to check with the rangers to see what the conditions are like. Driving 1,000 miles to look at slush does not make for a happy vacation.

**Finding the site:** From Cedar City, drive east on UT 14 for about 18 miles to the junction of UT 148. The junction is well-marked TO CEDAR BREAKS. Take UT 148 for about 6 miles to the visitor center.

**For more information:** Cedar Breaks National Monument, PO Box 749, Cedar City, UT 84720; (801) 586-9451

## Fish Springs National Wildlife Refuge

Far out in the west desert lie almost 18,000 acres of marshland. In a harsh and arid land that looks as though there wouldn't be a drop of water in 18,000 miles, this truly shows that Mother Nature has a sense of humor. Right on the Pacific Flyway, this anomaly is a stopover point and nesting area for ducks, swans, Canada geese, great blue herons, snowy egrets, avocets, and many others. There is also an abundance of mammals, reptiles, and amphibians.

This whole strange, out-of-place site is possible because of the many warm springs that seep through an old fault. First used by native peoples in pre-Columbian times, the area has also been used by the Pony Express riders. In the early twentieth century, the Lincoln Highway, the nation's first transcontinental highway, came through what is now the refuge. Stretches of this old highway are still visible on the refuge.

There is no camping allowed at Fish Springs, but there is a picnic ground, and you can pick up a brochure at the information booth and drive an 11.5-mile loop around the refuge.

**Finding the site:** From Obsidian Hill, continue on the marked road to Fish Springs. If you're hunting at Gold Hill, continue on to Callao and east on the Old Pony Express Road to Fish Springs. If you are collecting wonderstone at Vernon, you can take the Old Pony Express Road west to Fish Springs.

## Grand Staircase–Escalante National Monument

Grand Staircase–Escalante National Monument protects 1.9 million acres of land in southern Utah. There are three main regions: the Grand Staircase, the Kaiparowits Plateau, and the Canyons of the Escalante—all of which are administered by the BLM as part of the National Landscape Conservation System. President Bill Clinton designated the area as a national monument in 1996 using his authority under the Antiquities Act. Slightly larger in area than the state of Delaware, Grand Staircase–Escalante encompasses the largest land area of all US national monuments.

The monument stretches from the towns of Big Water, Glendale, and Kanab on the southwest to the towns of Escalante and Boulder on the northeast.

The western part of the monument is dominated by the Paunsaugunt Plateau and the Paria River and is adjacent to Bryce Canyon National Park.

**Finding the site:** You can find many areas to get into this site. When we were there, we found that the best scenic route through the area was to follow UT 89 to the intersection of UT 12 south of Panguitch, Utah. This road will take you through Escalante and Boulder, Utah. When you take the turnoff in Boulder, the Burr Trail heads east for 26 miles over to Bullfrog Marina at Lake Powell. This road is paved for most of the way. This is one of the most scenic areas of the Grand Staircase–Escalante.

**For more information:** Grand Staircase–Escalante National Monument, Kanab Headquarters, 669 South Highway 89A, Kanab, Utah 84741; (435) 644-1200

## Lake Powell

Where once the mighty Colorado River wound its tortuous way through the deep gorges of remote and beautiful Glen Canyon, there now exists the second-largest man-made lake in the United States. The 186-mile-long lake is a triumph of engineering, but after some thirty years or more, it is still a matter of controversy between those to whom electric power, irrigation, and recreation are primary and those to whom the protection of nature's wonders takes precedence over the construction feats of man.

The arguments go on, but the fact is that we now have a lake with 1,960 miles of shoreline and enough bays and coves (formerly side canyons) to keep a boater busy for a lifetime. Deep beneath the surface there are probably rock-hound sites that would have kept us all busy for several lifetimes. Ah well! As the saying goes, "That's all water over the rockhound site."

The lake is in such a remote area that only a few roads go to it. Most of the exploration has to be done by boat. There are some roads near a few of the sites in this book, though. If you go to Fry Canyon to look for petrified wood, you will cross the northern end of the lake at Hite Crossing. There are several viewpoints along the road where you can get an idea of the size of the lake. From the Escalante area you can take the Hole in the Rock Road to the lake at Hole in the Rock. If you go to Shootering Canyon and Hansen Creek, you can continue on UT 276 to Bullfrog Marina.

If you are near any of these sites and have never seen Lake Powell, you really should run over and take a look. Even if you are not a boater, you will be glad you did. You can even rent a houseboat and float around dreaming of the gemstones that await you only a thousand feet or so below. Scuba anyone?

## Little Sahara Recreation Area

Located between Eureka and Delta are 60,000 acres of sand dunes and sagebrush to play in. This sounds like a great place to take your cat on vacation.

All this sand started life about 10,000 years ago as part of the southern shoreline beaches of ancient Lake Bonneville, which lie about 150 miles to the southwest. As Lake Bonneville began to recede, the sands were blown northeastward at about 18 inches a year. There was nothing to stop the movement across the barren desert until the sand reached Sand Mountain. As the winds reached the mountain, they were deflected upward, which caused the sand to drop and pile up into dunes.

Today the sands that began as an ancient shoreline are used primarily for recreation. There are areas for dune buggies, motorcycles, and four-wheel-drive vehicles to play in. There are also areas set aside for children, and more than 9,000 acres have been designated as a nature study area. There are several campgrounds that are open year-round. There is a nominal entry fee, but the fee includes use of the campgrounds.

**Finding the site:** From Eureka, drive south on US 6 for 17 miles; take the well-marked road to the right for another 4.5 miles to the dunes. From Delta, drive north on US 6 for 32 miles to the turnoff.

**For more information:** Bureau of Land Management, 15 East 500, Fillmore, UT 84631; (801) 743-6811

## Mountain Meadows Massacre Site

Just 4.7 miles from the turnoff to Central (Site 1) is a monument to one of the saddest incidents in the history of the West—the Mountain Meadows Massacre. This pleasant valley, which was far lusher in the 1800s than it is today, was used by those traveling on the old Spanish and California trails. Those heading west used it as a last stopover before they faced the heat of the desert, while those heading east used it to rest and recuperate from their long trek.

In the fall of 1857, a wagon train of emigrants from Arkansas and Missouri were traveling the southern route to California. Evidently, they had made some offensive remarks to the Mormons as they went through the area around Cedar City. The story gets a little fuzzy, and the whole truth may never be known, but a group of Mormons and local Indians attacked the train at Mountain Meadows and killed about 120 of the party. Only small children too young to tell the story were spared. When federal authorities tried to investigate, the close-knit Mormon communities hindered their attempts to see that justice was done. Only John D. Lee was ever brought to justice, and it took nearly twenty years and two trials to do it.

This road is gravel most of the way, but it has some of the best scenery in the state.

Today there is a nice road, a parking area, and a fine monument that looks a little like a miniature Vietnam Wall with the names of those killed and a description of the incident. It is sad to look over this peaceful valley and contemplate what horror happened here so long ago. It is a piece of history, though, and worth seeing if you are in the area.

**Finding the site:** From the turnoff to Site 1 on UT 18, drive 4.7 miles to the well-marked turnoff to the site.

## Natural Bridges National Monument

Natural Bridges National Monument lies in a remote area of southeastern Utah in a spot that makes you wonder how anyone ever discovered it. We have to credit those old-timers who wandered through the vastness of the West for bringing back tales of natural wonders that excited the imaginations of the public. In this case it was a prospector by the name of Cass Hite, who told of the huge stone bridges he had seen in his travels. Those with a spirit of adventure made their way to the bridges, and in 1904 *National Geographic* magazine sent an expedition to the site. In 1908 President Theodore Roosevelt declared the area a national monument. The federal government then changed the names of the bridges to the current Hopi Indian names, even though the Hopi never lived there. I rest my case.

Although it is remote, the monument is easy to get to on paved highways. There is a fine visitor center and a 9-mile loop drive from which you can view the three bridges. There is also a campground at the monument that will accommodate RVs up to 21 feet. Vehicles longer than this can use the overflow area.

The largest of the bridges is Sipapu. The name is Hopi for the gateway from which the Hopi believe they entered the world. Sipapu is 220 feet high and has a span of 268 feet. There are two hiking trails from which to view the bridge. One is about halfway down into the canyon; the other goes clear to the bottom. Round-trip to the bottom is about 1.2 miles and is probably the best place from which to realize the size of the bridge.

The middle bridge is Kachina, the name for the Hopi spirits. It has a span of 204 feet and a height of 210 feet. A trail of about 1.5 miles round-trip goes to the bottom of the canyon. There are pictographs near the bottom of the trail.

The third of the bridges is Owachomo. The name means "flat rock mound" and is named for a rock outcropping nearby. Owachomo is the smallest of the three, with a height of 106 feet and a span of 180 feet. It also has the shortest and easiest trail to the bottom. The round-trip is only 0.5 mile.

There are also some very interesting Anasazi ruins to be seen here. Whether you favor the bridges or the ruins, if you are collecting at the Fry Canyon site, you really must drive the few extra miles, see some rare sights, and get some prize-winning pictures to dazzle the relatives and neighbors back home.

**Finding the site:** From Fry Canyon, drive southeast on UT 95 for about 26 miles to the well-marked turnoff to the monument.

**For more information:** Natural Bridges National Monument, PO Box 1, Lake Powell, UT 84533; (801) 259-5174

## Timpanogos Cave National Monument

From the visitor center on the Alpine Scenic Loop just north of Provo in American Fork Canyon, a twisting trail climbs 1,065 feet in 1.5 miles to the entrance to Timpanogos Cave. If you wore good hiking shoes or boots and brought along a jacket or sweater, you are about to tour an outstanding cave. Since the site was declared a national monument in 1922, hundreds of thousands of visitors have made the trek up the mountainside and toured the cave. Actually, Timpanogos is three separate caves. They have been connected by man-made tunnels but retain their own unique features.

Hansen Cave is the first cave on the tour. It was discovered by Martin Hansen, who then owned the land, in 1877. Nearly all the formations once here have been taken—some by tourists in the early days and some by those who sold them as souvenirs.

Middle Cave was discovered in 1922. It is narrow, with a high ceiling that reaches 125 feet in places. This cave was originally entered from the top. Explorers lowered themselves down with ropes. Because of the drafts, the opening in the top was sealed when the tunnel was completed. The formations in Middle Cave are almost all intact and range in color from white to yellow to shades of brown and tan.

Timpanogos Cave proper is the third of the three and is connected to Middle Cave by a 190-foot-long man-made tunnel. This is probably the most beautiful of the three caves. Formations in here have names like the Dove's Nest, the Reclining Camel, Mother Earth's Lace Curtains, and the Chocolate Fountain. Another formation, the Heart of Timpanogos, is illuminated from behind and bears a striking resemblance to the human heart.

If you visit the cave, and haven't already done so, you might as well continue over the Alpine Scenic Loop. If you can arrange the trip in the fall when the leaves are changing color, you will be glad you did.

**Finding the site:** From Provo, drive north on I-15 to exit 287 north of Lehi. Take UT 92 for 9 miles to the visitor center. From the Salt Lake area, drive south on I-15 and take the same exit to UT 92.

**For more information:** Timpanogos Cave National Monument, RR 3, PO Box 200, American Fork, UT 84003; (801) 756-5238

### Zion National Park

Zion, along with Bryce Canyon, is almost synonymous with Utah. Both are beautiful, but both are so easily accessible that crowding is a concern. This obviously poses no problem for many people, since they keep coming and smile while they are here. Utah has such vast areas of beautiful rock formations, though, that a little creativity with the map and a four-wheel-drive vehicle or pickup will get you to some gorgeous spots where you will be all alone.

Even if you are a loner, you really have to see Zion at least once. In fact, it would be impossible to see it all in one visit. You can take the auto tours on paved roads and get a feel for the place, but you will have to don your hiking boots to do it justice. This is a year-round park, so think about coming in the off-season. Snow may be a problem in the high country in winter, but there are plenty of trails that are open all winter.

Zion is a natural for those who may be traveling between Hurricane Mesa and Mount Carmel. You can drive through the park and take in some of the sights on the way. Be sure to take the ride up Zion Canyon. You will be driving next to cliffs that rise as high as 2,400 feet above you. It is truly awe inspiring. Even if you don't have time to hike, you will see spectacular red-rock formations and some fantastic scenery.

**Finding the site:** From Saint George, drive north on I-15 for about 7 miles to exit 16. Follow UT 9 through Hurricane and La Verkin to the park entrance. From the junction of US 89 and UT 9 at Mount Carmel Junction, take UT 9 west to the park entrance.

**For more information:** Zion National Park, Springdale, UT 84767; (801) 772-3256

These sites have been set up so that you can get the most out of your day, weekend, or week as you go out to rock hunt. Be safe and have fun and enjoy the rockhounding that Utah has to offer.

—Gary Warren

# Map Legend

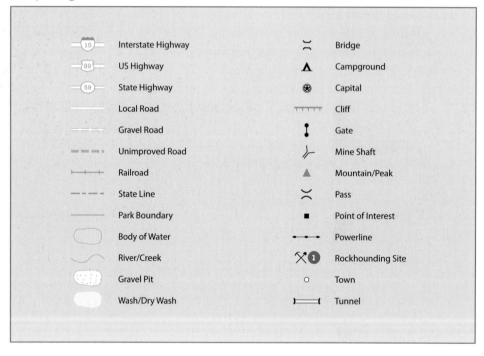

| | | | | |
|---|---|---|---|---|
| | Interstate Highway | | | Bridge |
| | US Highway | | | Campground |
| | State Highway | | | Capital |
| | Local Road | | | Cliff |
| | Gravel Road | | | Gate |
| | Unimproved Road | | | Mine Shaft |
| | Railroad | | | Mountain/Peak |
| | State Line | | | Pass |
| | Park Boundary | | | Point of Interest |
| | Body of Water | | | Powerline |
| | River/Creek | | | Rockhounding Site |
| | Gravel Pit | | | Town |
| | Wash/Dry Wash | | | Tunnel |

# SOUTH UTAH

# 1. Central: Agate

Road leading from power plant to site 1

**Land type:** Cedar-covered hills
**Elevation:** 5,292 feet
**GPS:** N37 25.032' / W113 38.471'
**Best seasons:** Spring through fall
**Land manager:** Dixie National Forest
**Materials:** Agate, jasper
**Tool:** Rock hammer
**Vehicle:** Any
**Special attraction:** Mountain Meadows Massacre Site
**Accommodations:** Camping at Pine Valley Recreation Area and Baker Dam Campground; motels and RV parking in St. George area
**Finding the site:** From the intersection of St. George Boulevard and UT 18 in St. George, drive northwest on UT 18 for 25.7 miles to the Pine Valley Recreation Area turnoff. This is the site of the tiny town of Central. At the intersection by Central, turn left onto a gravel road and proceed west for just under 1 mile. Just before you

# Site 1

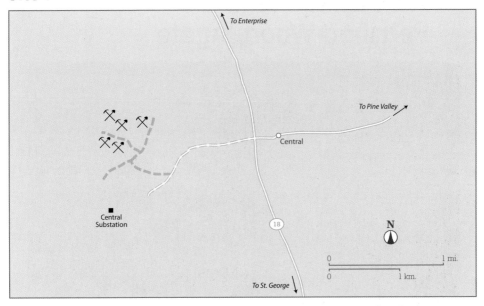

To Enterprise

To Pine Valley

Central

Central
Substation

18

N

0            1 mi.

0            1 km.

To St. George

reach a dead end at the Central power substation, you will see a dirt forest road to your right. If you miss the road and end up at the substation, just backtrack to the first dirt road to the left. Follow this road for 0.3 mile. Park anywhere and start hunting along both sides of the road.

## Rockhounding

There is quite a bit of both agate and jasper at this site, but finding the good stuff will take a little hunting. Be patient and you will be rewarded. Be sure to look on both sides of the road. There is a lot of territory to cover out here, so take your time and explore as much of it as you can.

When you finish collecting, you might want to go back to UT 18 and drive north 4.7 miles to the well-marked Mountain Meadows Massacre Site. It is just a short way off the road to the monument, and it is well worth seeing where this tragedy in both Utah and human history took place.

# 2. Hurricane Mesa: Petrified Wood, Agate

Hurricane Mesa

**Land type:** High mesa
**Elevation:** 5,021 feet
**GPS:** N37 14.472' / W113 12.486'
**Best seasons:** Spring through fall
**Land manager:** Utah Division of State Lands
**Materials:** Agate, jasper, petrified wood
**Tool:** Rock hammer
**Vehicle:** Any
**Special attractions:** Old rocket track and test site
**Accommodations:** Motels; RV parking, camping in the St. George area; camping at Zion National Park

## Site 2

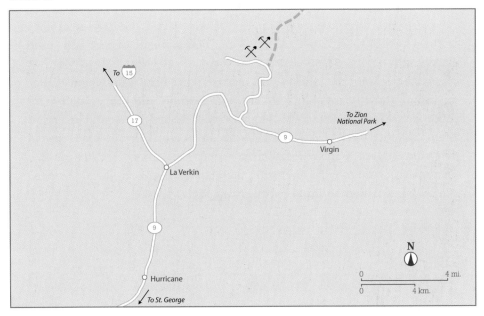

**Finding the site:** From the town of La Verkin, take UT 9 east for 4.9 miles. The mesa is clearly visible to the north, and a road goes off to the left heading toward the mesa. The forest sign that used to be at this intersection is gone, and the road is a little hard to see, so keep a sharp eye out. This highway is the route to Zion National Park, so there is a lot of traffic. If you miss the turnoff, just proceed until you can turn around and backtrack to the road to the mesa. The road is paved most of the way, but the unpaved sections are fine for passenger cars. At 3.4 miles along the road, you will be on top of the mesa. A dead-end road goes left to the gates of the old test track, and a dirt road goes right toward Smith Mesa. Follow the Smith Mesa road for 0.2 mile, and park off the road.

## Rockhounding

Some nice material can be picked up in this area. Look for open spaces where the gravel is evident, and search there. This is a big mesa, so be sure to roam around. I have had good luck near the base of the red cliffs, but it takes some walking to get there. There is some private property up on the mesa now, so be sure to heed any posting. Be especially careful not to enter the test track area. It may be tempting, but it is a great big no–no!

To look around this remote mesa today, it is difficult to visualize the activity that took place here in the 1950s. Unknown by the vast majority of Americans, and forgotten by most in the US Air Force, is the fascinating story of the Hurricane Mesa test track and the development of the high-speed ejection seat.

By the time of the Korean War, military jet fighters were flying at near supersonic speeds at high altitudes. The pilot ejection seats of the day had not kept pace with other aircraft developments, and about 80 percent of the pilots attempting high-speed bailouts were either injured or killed. It was clear that a new type of seat was needed, but the problem for the researchers was that such speeds could only be reached in flight; that was dangerous to personnel and risked both lives and very expensive aircraft.

# 3. Gooseberry Mesa: Petrified Wood

Gooseberry Mesa at 9 miles

**Land type:** Base of cliffs
**Elevation:** 4,447 feet
**GPS:** N37 7.120' / W113 10.381'
**Best seasons:** Spring through fall
**Land manager:** BLM
**Material:** Petrified wood
**Tool:** Rock hammer
**Vehicle:** Any
**Special attraction:** Zion National Park
**Accommodations:** Motels; private RV parking and camping in Hurricane; public camping in Zion National Park
**Finding the site:** From the town of Hurricane, drive southeast on UT 59 for 9 miles. You will see several dirt tracks leading over to the base of the high cliffs to

## Sites 3–4

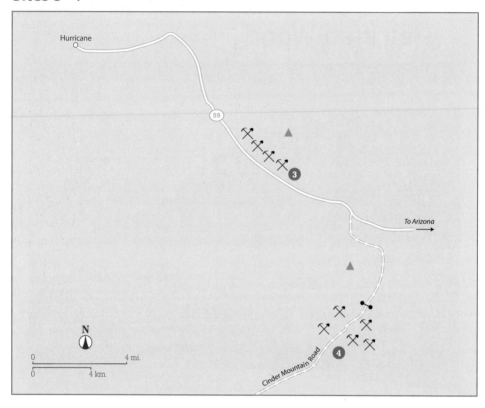

your left. Take any of them, and get as close to the base as you can. Park and hunt along the base of the cliffs.

## Rockhounding

Material here is scarce, but we did find some very nice specimens of wood with quartz crystals on one side and nice bark definition on the other. I wouldn't recommend driving a long way to visit this site, but I included it because it is right next to the highway and a good place to stretch your legs if you are passing by. Who knows what you might find while stretching?

# 4. Cinder Mountain: Petrified Wood

Specimen from Cinder Mountain

(See map on page 38.)

**Land type:** Cedar-covered mesa

**Elevation:** 5,207 feet

**GPS:** N37 4.463' / W113 8.637'

**Best seasons:** Spring through fall

**Land manager:** BLM

**Material:** Petrified wood

**Tool:** Rock hammer

**Vehicle:** Any

**Special attraction:** Zion National Park

**Accommodations:** Motels; private RV parking and camping in Hurricane

**Finding the site:** From Hurricane, go southeast on UT 59 for 13.6 miles. Turn south onto Cinder Mountain Road. The road makes a 90-degree turn to the left at 0.23 mile. At 0.8 mile from the turn, make a 90-degree turn to the right. Follow this

The road that leads to Cinder Mountain

road for a total of 3.1 miles from UT 59. Just before you get to the parking area, at 2.8 miles, there is a large pit up next to Cinder Mountain, where there is now a gravel pit. Park your vehicle just beyond the cattleguard, and hunt all over the mesa. We did not find a lot of material at this point in 2012.

## Rockhounding

This is a very large area that has been hunted for years, so allow yourself plenty of time for exploration. Most of what we found was just silicified wood with nice definition but no color or jewelry potential. Much nice agatized wood has been found here, though, so look carefully and do a little digging if you want the best.

# 5. Kolob Reservoir: Fossils

Fossils are still found in this area.

**Land type:** Road cut
**Elevation:** 7,833 feet
**GPS:** N37 22.583' / W113 4.138'
**Best seasons:** Late spring through early fall
**Land manager:** Dixie National Forest
**Material:** Pelecypod fossils
**Tool:** Rock hammer
**Vehicle:** Any
**Special attractions:** Kolob Reservoir; Zion National Park
**Accommodations:** Motels; private RV parking and camping in Cedar City; public RV parking and camping in Zion National Park
**Finding the site:** Begin this trip at the town of Virgin, on UT 9 between Hurricane and the Zion National Park entrance. From Virgin, take the Kolob Road from the center of town north for 18.5 miles to a huge road cut on the right. At

# Site 5

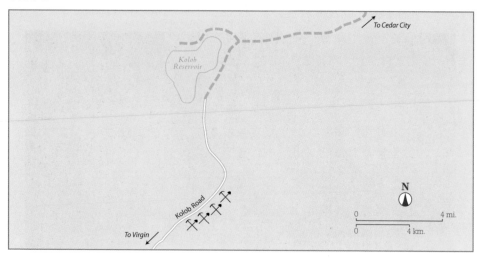

approximately 7.6 miles there is an intersection; the road goes to the right. (Don't keep going straight like we did for a few miles.) At 18.5 miles there is a wide parking area at the base of the cut. This is a good place for the kids, since you are well off the road and there is not a lot of traffic.

## Rockhounding

These are not the greatest fossils in the world, but they are plentiful, and a little searching will turn up some nice ones. They are in a gray limestone, but so many are exposed that you won't have to split them if you don't want to.

For a really beautiful trip, continue on past Kolob Reservoir and down into Cedar City. The road is dirt from the reservoir and can be impassable in wet weather. If it is dry, however, the family car will make it okay.

# 6. Cedar City: Minerals

You cannot miss the tailings piles at this site.

**Land types:** Hills; tailings piles
**Elevation:** 6,207 feet
**GPS:** N37 36.754' / W113 24.171'
**Best seasons:** Spring through fall
**Land manager:** Private
**Material:** Mineral specimens
**Tool:** Rock hammer
**Vehicle:** Any
**Special attraction:** Old Iron Town Ruins
**Accommodations:** Motels; public and private RV parking and camping in Cedar City area
**Finding the site:** From Cedar City, drive west on UT 56 for 20 miles. You will see huge tailings piles on the right. Several dirt roads lead to the tailings. This area is now operational again, so be careful where you hunt, as there is private property in this area.

# Site 6

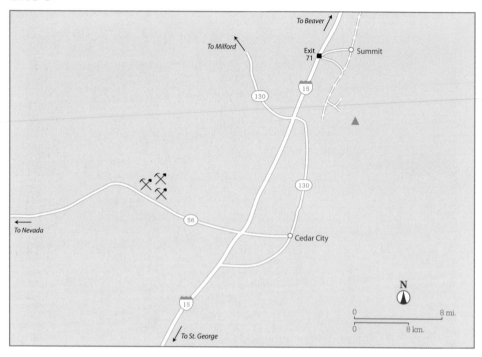

## Rockhounding

These mines were operated for many years, and the tailings piles are numerous and large. Among the minerals that have been found here are pyrite, hematite, barite, cinnabar, and some amethyst. We found a little, but we didn't have a lot of time. If you can stay awhile, you are bound to find some nice specimens. Remember, though, there are tons of rock to sort through. You may kiss quite a few frogs before you find a prince, but there are princes in there.

The status of collecting seems to be open with the exception of one area that is still being worked. We checked with the chamber of commerce and were assured that collectors are welcome.

# 7. Modena Canyon: Obsidian, Chalcedony

These pieces were lying on the side of the road.

**Land type:** Rolling hills
**Elevation:** 6,040 feet
**GPS:** N37 52.521' / W113 56.533'
**Best seasons:** Spring and fall
**Land manager:** BLM
**Materials:** Obsidian, chalcedony
**Tool:** Rock hammer
**Vehicle:** Any
**Special attractions:** None
**Accommodations:** Motels; public and private RV parking and camping in the Cedar City area
**Finding the site:** From Cedar City, drive west on UT 56 for 51 miles to the town of Modena. Modena is off the highway to the left. Do not turn into town, but continue across the bridge over the railroad tracks. Just past the end of the bridge, Modena Canyon Road goes right. Follow the road for 5.5 miles, and park off the road.

# Site 7

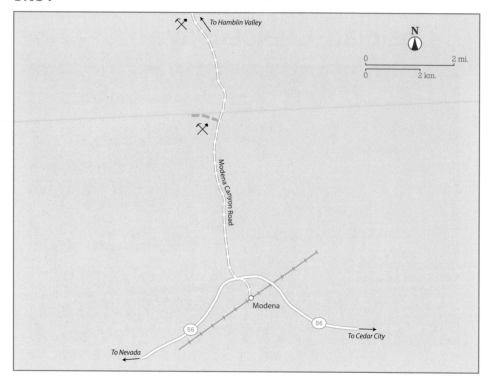

## Rockhounding:

The hillside to the left is covered with obsidian chips. A little searching and some digging will probably turn up some nice-size pieces. We found nice nodules alongside the road where the road grader had pushed up a little berm. This site is a long way from civilization, so I certainly wouldn't encourage anyone to come here just for the obsidian. On the other hand, if you are traveling between tedium and apathy and need a break, this is a good place to take one.

After you have had your break and are heading back to the highway, you might want to stop at a spot 2.3 miles from the obsidian site. There are the remains of a road here, and if you search the hillside to the south of the road, you can find some nice little pieces of botryoidal chalcedony. I think they make nice little display pieces, and children love them. Many of them also make great looking wire-wrapped pins or pendants.

# 8. Brian Head: Agate

This large rock of agate weighs in at more than 200 pounds, or over your weight limit.

**Land type:** Mountains
**Elevation:** 10,351 feet
**GPS:** N37 40.372' / W112 50.072'
**Best seasons:** Spring through fall
**Land manager:** Dixie National Forest
**Material:** Agate
**Tool:** Rock hammer
**Vehicle:** Any
**Special attraction:** Cedar Breaks National Monument
**Accommodations:** Motels at Cedar City and Brian Head; private RV parking and camping in Cedar City area; public RV parking and camping at Cedar Breaks National Monument; national forest camping at Navajo Lake and Duck Creek
**Finding the site:** From the visitor center at Cedar Breaks National Monument, go north for 5.7 miles. At this point, take the dirt road to the right. The road is marked TO BRIAN HEAD PEAK. At approximately 0.5 mile the road crosses a bridge over a little

This gully is at the first bridge on the road to the top of the mountain.

creek. Park off the road, and hunt to the left along the banks and in the creek. This area is now a ski area and is closed to rockhounding in winter. During summer, there are places to hunt in the area.

## Rockhounding

Although it is usually fractured, this is some of the prettiest agate you will ever see. Work around the fractures, and make yourself some trophy winners. I am a sucker for this material and have a backyard full to prove it. I must not be the only one, though. One summer Cora, our sons Bill and Richard, and I were poking around the creek when a motor home with two visitors from New Zealand pulled up.

Agate is in the bottom of the gully.

## Sites 8–9

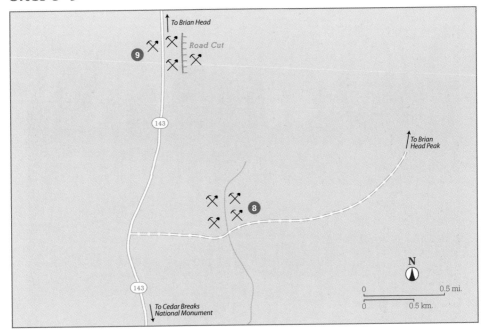

They were so impressed that by the time they left, they had every storage space and the bunks of their motor home filled with "fractured" agate.

When Sally and I visited in July 2013, the little stream was running and there were pieces of agate everywhere. I walked up the creek and found boulders of agate lying in the streambed.

If the road is dry, you can continue on up to the top of 11,307-foot Brian Head Peak. This was originally called Monument Peak but was changed to honor William Jennings Bryan. (Although it's not much of an honor to have your name misspelled.) From the lookout at the top, you can see much of southern Utah and on a clear day can see into Arizona and Nevada. You might even see some agate you missed down below.

# 9. Cedar Breaks: Agate

Park and walk to this cut on the side of the road.

(See map on page 49.)
**Land type:** Road cut
**Elevation:** 10,244 feet
**GPS:** N37 40.591' / W112 50.564'
**Best season:** Summer
**Land manager:** Dixie National Forest
**Material:** Agate
**Tool:** Rock hammer
**Vehicle:** Any
**Special attraction:** Cedar Breaks National Monument
**Accommodations:** Motels in Cedar City and Brian Head; private RV parking and camping in Cedar City; public camping and RV parking at Cedar Breaks National Monument; national forest camping at Navajo Lake and Duck Creek

**Finding the site:** From the visitor center at Cedar Breaks National Monument, go north on UT 143 for 6.6 miles to a large road cut on the right. There is a wide parking area on the left side of the road. Park, and hunt in and above the cut.

## Rockhounding

This is an extension of the agate beds at the Brian Head creek site (site 8). The nice part is that the big road machinery has already done the heavy lifting for us.

# 10. Twisted Forest: Agate

Watch for this sign to get to the Twisted Forest Trail.

**Land type:** Mountains
**Elevation:** 9,535 at parking area
**GPS:** N37 41.101' / W112 53.443'
**Best seasons:** Spring through fall
**Land manager:** Dixie National Forest
**Material:** Agate
**Tool:** Rock hammer
**Vehicle:** High-clearance
**Special attractions:** Cedar Breaks National Monument; bristlecone pine forest
**Accommodations:** Motels at Cedar City and Brian Head; private RV parking and camping in Cedar City area; public RV parking and camping at Cedar Breaks National Monument; national forest camping at Navajo Lake and Duck Creek
**Finding the site:** From the visitor center at Cedar Breaks National Monument, drive north on UT 143 for 7 miles to the junction with Sugarloaf Mountain Road. Follow

# Site 10

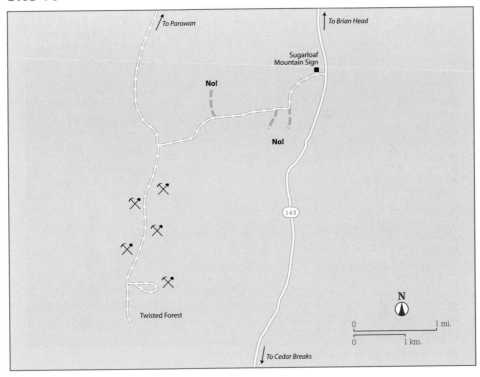

this road for 3.4 miles from the highway, where you will find a dirt road going left. This is the road to the Twisted Forest Trailhead. Drive in, and park on the loop.

## Rockhounding

There is a large white patch on the east side of the parking loop where you can find some really nice colorful pieces of agate. Look on the flats and in the road too. On the way back, look at the road berms that the grader has turned up. There is a lot of agate in them.

Before you leave the Twisted Forest parking area, you may want to take the short hike out to see the bristlecone pines. This is one of the oldest living plant species, and they are truly fascinating. If you walk to the end of the area, you will have a fantastic view of Cedar Breaks. Be sure to hang on to the kids. The view is from the top of the cliffs. I won't say how far the drop is, but this book would probably be in its fourth printing before you hit bottom.

# 11. Turnout: Agate

At the turnout you can see the creek at the bottom of the hill.

**Land type:** Mountain meadow
**Elevation:** 9,651 feet
**GPS:** N37 39.508' / W112 44.834'
**Best seasons:** Spring through fall
**Land manager:** Dixie National Forest
**Material:** Agate
**Tool:** Rock hammer
**Vehicle:** Any
**Special attraction:** Cedar Breaks National Monument
**Accommodations:** Motels in Cedar City and Brian Head; private RV parking and camping in Cedar City area; public RV parking and camping at Cedar Breaks National Monument; national forest camping at Navajo Lake and Duck Creek
**Finding the site:** From the visitor center in Cedar Breaks National Monument, drive 4.3 miles to the intersection of UT 143 and UT 148. Go east toward Panguitch

## Site 11

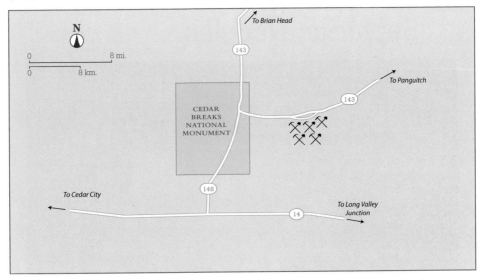

for 4.6 miles. You will see a gravel turnout on the right side of the road. Park at the turnout, and hunt in the meadow that runs down to the creek. The turnout will be just after mile marker 23.

## Rockhounding

This agate is similar to that at Brian Head (site 8) and Cedar Breaks (site 9). It is scattered all over the meadow. If you visit during the growing season, you may have to search a little harder, but the agate is there. Look for bare spots to start your search.

# 12. Mount Carmel: Septarian Nodules

Septarian nodule, Orderville, Utah

**Land type:** Hills
**Elevation:** 5,200 feet
**GPS:** Site location provided by rock shop
**Best seasons:** Spring through fall (impassable when wet)
**Land manager:** Private claims
**Material:** Septarian nodules
**Tools:** Rock hammer, shovel
**Vehicle:** High-clearance recommended
**Special attraction:** Zion National Park
**Accommodations:** Motels at Hatch and Mount Carmel Junction; private RV parking and camping at Hatch and Glendale
**Finding the site:** This is probably the most unusual site in this book. We are sending you first to a rock shop rather than a site. The owners of Joe's Rock Shop

# Site 12

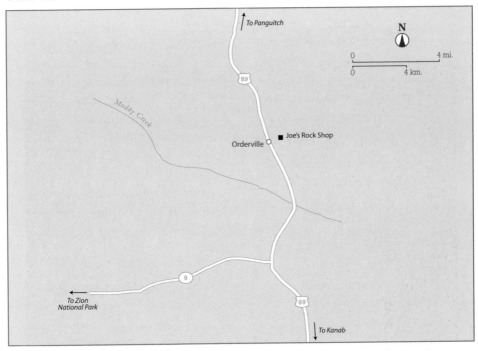

in Orderville own some of the famous claims along Muddy Creek. They do not prohibit collecting on their claims, nor do they charge a fee for collecting. All they ask is that you check in with them first and get instructions and a map.

The shop is in Orderville, which is on US 89 just a few miles north of the intersection of UT 9, the main route to Zion National Park. In talking with an older gentleman in Alton, I discovered that this area is probably one of the best sites to collect septarian nodules. He said that Alton, which is just up the road, is now a closed area and that there were not many (septarian nodules) left in the area.

## Rockhounding

The nodules are found along the steep banks of Muddy Creek. The nice part about this site is that the heavy lifting has been done for us. All the overburden has been removed, and little digging is necessary. The nodules range in size from golf ball to soccer ball. Bigger is not necessarily better, so don't overlook those little guys. Also, don't try to break them on-site. You will just end up with a lot of pieces to find uses for. If you find some decent broken pieces, take them along for projects, but don't break your own. You might easily destroy a real winner.

# 13. Casto Canyon: Agate

Agate is lying all over the ground at this site.

**Land type:** Low cedar-covered hill
**Elevation:** 7,042 feet
**GPS:** N37 47.124' / W112 20.352'
**Best seasons:** Spring through fall
**Land manager:** BLM
**Material:** Agate
**Tool:** Rock hammer
**Vehicle:** Any
**Special attraction:** Bryce Canyon National Park
**Accommodations:** Motels; private RV parking and camping in Hatch and
Panguitch; national forest camping at Panguitch Lake
**Finding the site:** From the intersection of US 89 and UT 12 south of Panguitch,
drive north on US 89 for 2.5 miles. At this point an unmarked dirt road goes east.
Cross the river on a new concrete bridge, and follow the dirt road for 3.3 miles.

# Site 13

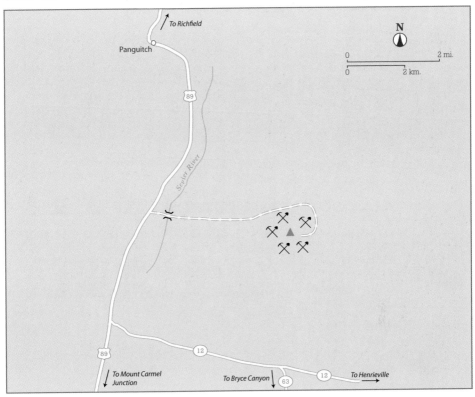

When we visited in 2013, there was a large parking area on the right. This is now known as Agate Hill.

## Rockhounding

This is probably the closest thing to a hill of solid agate I've ever seen. Unfortunately, much of it is without much pattern or figure. There is good material here, but you will have to be prepared to spend some time looking.

The wash to the east leads toward the red hills and is a good place to hunt when you tire of the hill. One year while I was wearing out boots hiking all over creation, Cora sat down on a rock in the middle of the wash, looked down at her feet, and picked up a perfect red sandstone snail pseudomorph. It was a twin of the tan one she had found at Red Canyon the day before. We searched both places thoroughly but never found another. You might keep an eye out for their relatives.

# SOUTHEAST UTAH

# 14. Sand Creek: Petrified Wood

**Land types:** High desert, hills
**Elevation:** 7,173 feet
**GPS:** N38 20.134' / W111 01.242'
**Best seasons:** Spring and fall
**Land manager:** Fishlake National Forest
**Material:** Petrified wood
**Tool:** Rock hammer
**Vehicle:** High-clearance
**Special attraction:** Capitol Reef National Park
**Accommodations:** Motels; private RV parking and camping in Torrey; public RV parking and camping in Capitol Reef National Park

## Site 14

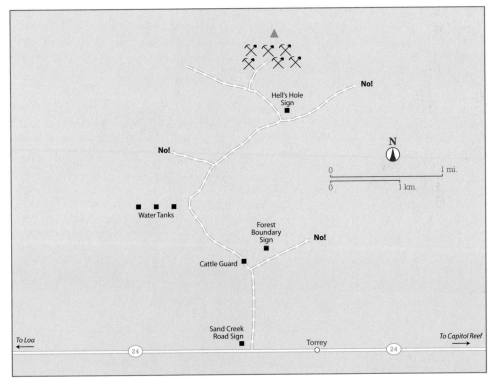

**Finding the site:** From the general store in the middle of Torrey, drive west for 0.6 mile to Sand Creek Road. Go north on Sand Creek Road for 0.8 mile to a fork. The road from here becomes very rough; four-wheel drive is suggested. Take the left fork, cross a cattleguard, and proceed 0.6 mile to three large water tanks on the left. At 0.2 mile beyond the water tanks, the road forks; keep right. At 0.7 mile from the fork, come to another fork. There is a sign for HELL'S HOLE on the left fork. Follow this for 0.2 mile, where a road exits to the right. Take this for another 0.2 mile, and park as close to the big red mountain as you can. Walk over, and hunt in the red clay at the foot of the cliffs.

## Rockhounding

This area is now in Dixie National Forest, and a permit is required to collect anything in the forest. Most of the wood has now been taken from this area, and what remains is hard to find. There are a few pieces lying here and there on the ground.

# 15. Blue Hills: Agate, Selenite Crystals

Here we're looking from the top of the hill down to the highway.

**Land types:** High desert, hills
**Elevation:** 4,694 feet
**GPS:** N38 21.906' / W110 53.447'
**Best seasons:** Spring and fall
**Land manager:** BLM
**Materials:** Agate, selenite crystals
**Tool:** Rock hammer
**Vehicle:** Any
**Special attractions:** Capitol Reef National Park; Glen Canyon National Recreation Area
**Accommodations:** Motels; private RV parking and camping in Hanksville; public RV parking and camping at Capitol Reef National Park
**Finding the site:** From the highway department shed at the west end of Hanksville, drive 10.3 miles west toward Capitol Reef National Park. At this point

# Site 15

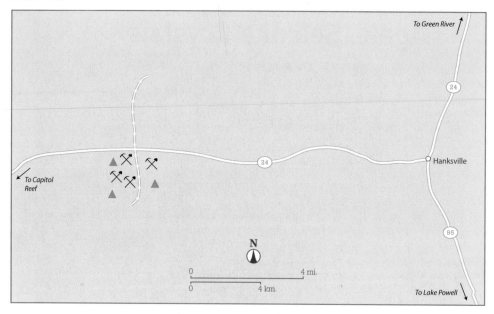

a gravel road heads right into the Swing Arm City off-highway-vehicle (OHV) area and a dirt road goes left. Take the left road for 0.2 mile to the top of a little hill, and park.

## Rockhounding

The hills here are covered with agate. A little walking will turn up some really pretty pieces. Most are not large but will cut into cabochons very nicely. You can also find a little agatized petrified wood and some nice selenite crystals.

The road continues into the hills, but we did not follow it. You might want to give it a try. This area is known for quality agate, and it is entirely possible that you will find it if you do a little exploring.

# 16. Caineville: Agate

There are some really nice pieces of agate in this area.

**Land type:** High desert
**Elevation:** 4,652 feet
**GPS:** N38 22.314' / W110 46.066'
**Best seasons:** Spring and fall
**Land manager:** BLM
**Material:** Agate
**Tool:** Rock hammer
**Vehicle:** Any
**Special attraction:** Capitol Reef National Park
**Accommodations:** Motels; private RV parking and camping in Hanksville and Torrey; public RV parking and camping in Capitol Reef National Park
**Finding the site:** From the highway department yard at the west end of Hanksville, at 18 miles there is a Rodeway Inn, where you can stay the night for this area. Drive west on UT 24 for 18.1 miles. At this point a road goes right to

# Site 16

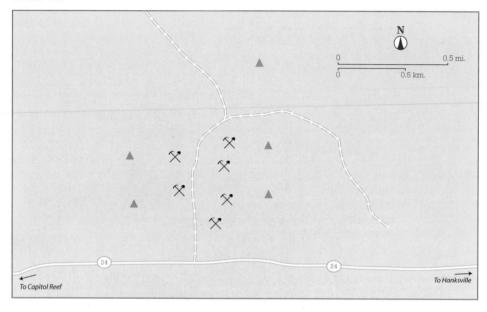

a wide flat area surrounded by gray hills. Drive in, and park near the foot of the hills. There are signs posted for NO VEHICLE TRAVEL IN AREA, so be careful of where you pull off. At 18.3 miles there is a gravel road on the right that goes into the North Caineville Reef area. Check this area also for some good Agate.

## Rockhounding

Hunt in the rocky areas at the foot of the hills. There is nice agate scattered among the black and brown volcanic rocks. All the hills have the same rocky formations. I didn't check out every one, but I bet they all contain agate.

# 17. Fossil Shell Hills: Devil's Toenails

Devil's toenails are in abundance at this site.

**Land types:** High desert, hills
**Elevation:** 5,063 feet
**GPS:** N38 19.860' / W111 26.763'
**Best seasons:** Spring and fall
**Land manager:** BLM
**Material:** Fossils
**Tools:** None
**Vehicle:** Any
**Special attraction:** Capitol Reef National Park
**Accommodations:** Motels; private RV parking and camping in Torrey; public RV parking and camping in Capitol Reef National Park
**Finding the site:** From the eastern boundary of Capitol Reef National Park on UT 24, drive east for 4.2 miles. At 0.6 mile you will see a sign to Notom; don't take this

# Sites 17–20

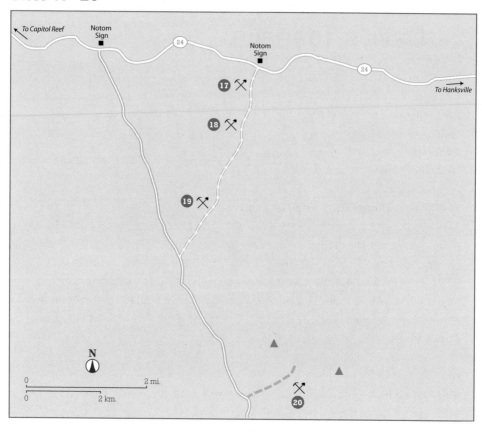

road. At 4.2 miles you will see a STOP sign on a dirt road coming from the right. This is the Old Notom Road. Follow it for 0.2 mile, and park on the right.

## Rockhounding

The bank to your right and all the hills for a mile or so around are literally paved with fossil shells. They are known locally as Henry Mountains shells or devil's toenails. When you have collected more toenails than you can use for the rest of your life, you can walk to the rocky areas on the hills and collect a little agate and quartzite. The agate is pretty well scattered, but some of it is very colorful.

# 18. Old Notom Road 1: Agate

(See map on page 68.)

**Land types:** High desert, hills

**Elevation:** 5,219 feet

**GPS:** N38 15.500' / W111 05.592'

**Best seasons:** Spring and fall

**Land manager:** BLM

**Material:** Agate

**Tool:** Rock hammer

**Vehicle:** Any

**Special attraction:** Capitol Reef National Park

**Accommodations:** Motels; private RV parking and camping at Torrey; public RV parking and camping in Capitol Reef National Park

**Finding the site:** From the eastern boundary of Capitol Reef National Park on UT 24, drive east for 4.2 miles. At 0.6 mile you will see a sign to Notom; don't take this road. At 4.2 miles you will see a STOP sign on a dirt road coming from the right. This is the Old Notom Road. Follow it for 1.2 miles, and park on the right side of the road.

## Rockhounding

You can collect some nice pieces of colorful agate here. Just walk over the hills and look for the rocky spots. There are also some nice selenite crystals here. They are not as plentiful as they are at the Hanksville site, but they are just as nice.

# 19. Old Notom Road 2:
## Agate, Calcite Crystals

This is a great site for hunting agate and calcite crystals.

(See map on page 68.)

**Land types:** High desert, hills

**Elevation:** 5,206 feet

**GPS:** N38 14.797' / W111 06.626'

**Best seasons:** Spring and fall

**Land manager:** BLM

**Materials:** Agate, calcite crystals

**Tool:** Rock hammer

**Vehicle:** Any

**Special attraction:** Capitol Reef National Park

**Accommodations:** Motels; private RV parking and camping in Torrey; public RV parking and camping in Capitol Reef National Park

**Finding the site:** From the eastern boundary of Capitol Reef National Park on UT 24, drive east for 4.2 miles. At 0.6 mile you will see a sign to Notom; don't take this

Park by the side of the road and just start looking.

road. At 4.2 miles you will see a STOP sign on a dirt road coming from the right. This is the Old Notom Road. Follow it for 3.7 miles, and park off the road. Hunt in the hills to the right and over to the deep gully on the left.

## Rockhounding
There are some very nice pieces of agate at this site. There are some larger pieces near the gully and on the hillsides. Scattered about are some pretty clear calcite crystals up to about 0.75 inch across.

# 20. Notom: Agate

This is the way to travel to most of the sites.

(See map on page 68.)

**Land types:** High desert, hills

**Elevation:** 5,489 feet

**GPS:** N38 12.081' / W111 05.828'

**Best seasons:** Spring and fall

**Land manager:** BLM

**Material:** Agate

**Tool:** Rock hammer

**Vehicle:** High-clearance

**Special attraction:** Capitol Reef National Park

**Accommodations:** Motels; private RV parking and camping at Torrey; public RV parking and camping in Capitol Reef National Park

**Finding the site:** From the eastern boundary of Capitol Reef National Park on UT 24, drive east for 4.2 miles. At 0.6 mile you will see a sign to Notom; don't take this

Agate like this can be found at this site.

road. At 4.2 miles you will see a STOP sign on a dirt road coming from the right. This is the Old Notom Road. Follow it for 4.5 miles to the intersection with the new paved Notom Road. Go left on the new road for 2.9 miles to a dirt road on the left. The road is a little hard to see, so keep your eyes peeled. If you start down a rather steep hill, you missed the turn. Follow the dirt road for 0.4 mile, and park off the road. Hunt on all the hilltops and washes to the right of the road.

## Rockhounding

There is agate all over the area, but the material near the road seems to be mostly a rather uninteresting milky white. The farther you walk, the more colorful the agate becomes. There are not huge pieces out here, but most are large enough for nice cabochons.

This is another area with roads going in all directions. To find the best, you too will have to go off in all directions.

# 21. The Badlands: Agate

Once you see this cattle guard, park your vehicle.

**Land type:** High desert
**Elevation:** 4,455 feet
**GPS:** N38 54.620' / W110 22.521'
**Best seasons:** Spring and fall
**Land manager:** BLM
**Material:** Agates
**Tool:** Rock hammer
**Vehicle:** Any
**Special attractions:** Interesting geological formations
**Accommodations:** Motels; private RV parking and camping in Hanksville and Torrey; public RV parking and camping in Capitol Reef National Park
**Finding the site:** From the intersection of UT 24 and UT 95 in Hanksville, drive west on UT 24 for 3.8 miles. You will see an unmarked dirt road going north. Follow this road as it winds around, climbs a little hill, and goes through a

## Site 21

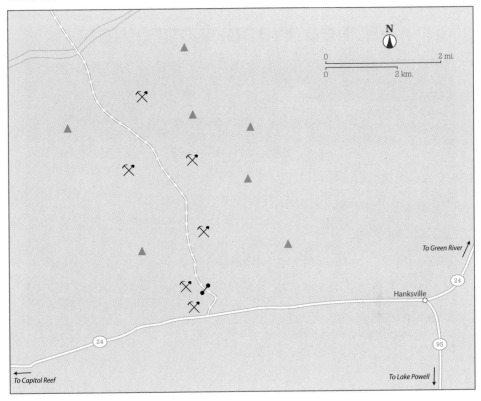

cattleguard. Park on the flat by the cattleguard, and hunt around both sides of the fence on both sides of the road for nice but small pieces of agate. When you have all you need, continue north on the road for about 5.5 miles.

## Rockhounding

All along the road you will be treated to some really fascinating geological formations. It is almost like a miniature Monument Valley. You can also pick up some small pieces of agate and jasper on both sides of the road. Look for patches of gravel, and go over and investigate. At the 5.5-mile point, you will come to a steep dip through a wash. If you are in the family car, it is time to turn around. There is supposed to be some agate in the wash, but I didn't find any. Maybe a little more walking would have done it.

# 22. Striped Mountain: Petrified Wood, Coprolites

This is the Striped Mountain that you are looking for.

**Land type:** Mountains
**Elevation:** 5,179 feet
**GPS:** N38 12.082' / W111 05.827'
**Best seasons:** Late spring and fall
**Land manager:** BLM
**Materials:** Coprolites, petrified wood
**Tools:** Rock hammer, digging tools
**Vehicle:** Four-wheel-drive
**Special attraction:** Lake Powell
**Accommodations:** Motels; private RV parking and camping in Hanksville
**Finding the site:** From the intersection of UT 24 and UT 95 in Hanksville, drive south on UT 95 for 20.4 miles to a dirt road going right. Follow this road for 3.7 miles to a fork, ignoring a fork going right at 1.4 miles. Go right at the fork and continue 0.6 mile. There is a BLM sign and a road going right. Keep left and proceed for 3 miles. This is a *very* rough road, and four-wheel drive is a must. At the 3-mile point, you will see a small red hill just off the road to your right and a large red-

# Site 22

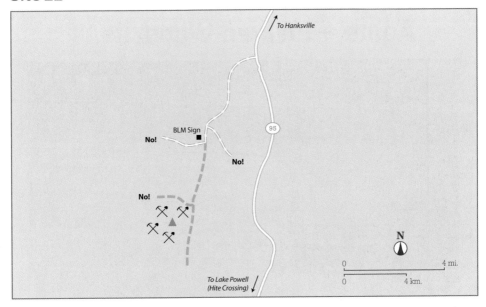

and-purple-striped hill just to the south on your right. Park on the flat, or drive between the hills and park on the flat.

## Rockhounding

There are petrified wood and agate behind the small hill and wood and coprolites around the back of the large hill. You might try hunting in the hills to the west beyond the flat. I have an idea there is a lot more material all around this area. Don't mistake concretions for petrified wood. The concretions in this area almost look like the wood; however, they do not have the grain in them that petrified wood does.

Some nice concreations and jasper can be found at this site.

# 23. Bullfrog Turnoff: Agate, Petrified Wood

Keep left at this fork.

**Land type:** Foothills
**Elevation:** 4,928 feet
**GPS:** N38 00.933' / W110 39.474'
**Best seasons:** Spring through fall
**Land manager:** BLM
**Materials:** Agate, petrified wood
**Tool:** Rock hammer
**Vehicle:** Any; four-wheel-drive for some
**Special attraction:** Lake Powell
**Accommodations:** Motels; private RV parking and camping in Hanksville; public camping at Star Springs Campground
**Finding the site:** From the intersection of UT 24 and UT 95 in Hanksville, drive south on UT 95 for 26 miles to the intersection with UT 276. Just 0.1 mile or so before the intersection, an unmarked dirt road at road marker 14900 goes

# Site 23

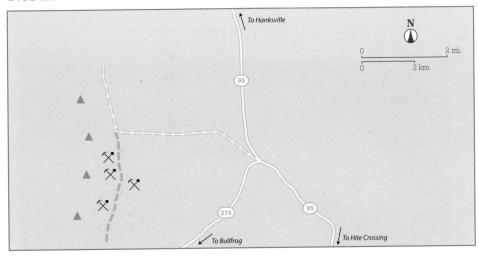

To Hanksville

N

0              2 mi.

0              2 km.

95

276

95

To Bullfrog

To Hite Crossing

to the right. Follow this road for 3.3 miles toward the cliffs. (GPS at this point is N38 02.290' / W110 37.376'.) The road forks, with the main road going right. You can park here and find a little petrified wood and some gray barite, but the best material is found along the left fork for 1 mile or so. This fork requires four-wheel drive.

## Rockhounding

The material along the left fork is small and scattered, but if you persist, you can find some really colorful pieces. If you like to walk and don't have four-wheel drive, there is a lot of country to cover. We found good material on both sides of the road.

Along with petrified wood, agate is also found in this area.

# 24. Shootering Canyon: Agate, Coprolites

Coprolites such as this can be found in this canyon.

**Land type:** Mountains
**Elevation:** 4,796 feet
**GPS:** N37 45.209' / W110 43.151'
**Best seasons:** Spring through fall
**Land manager:** BLM
**Materials:** Agate, coprolites
**Tool:** Rock hammer
**Vehicle:** High-clearance (four-wheel-drive recommended)
**Special attraction:** Lake Powell
**Accommodations**: Motels; private RV parking and camping in Hanksville; public RV parking and camping at Star Springs Campground
**Finding the site:** From the intersection of UT 24 and UT 95 in Hanksville, drive south on UT 95 for 26.2 miles to the junction with UT 276. Follow UT 276 south for 17.1 miles to the well-marked Star Springs turnoff. Go 3.4 miles on the Star Springs

# Sites 24–25

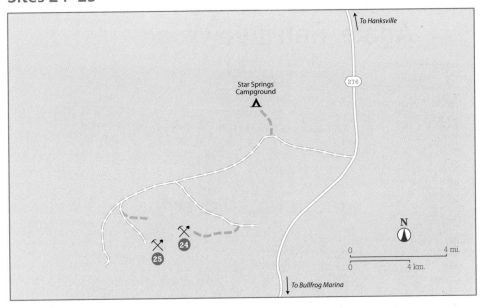

Road to a dirt road marked with a BLM sign on your left. Take this road for 1.9 miles, where you will come to a fork. Keep left at the fork and continue for another 2.5 miles to the Shootering Canyon turnoff on the left. Follow the Shootering Canyon Road for 3.6 miles. At this point you will see a yellow chimney-like structure on the hillside to your right. This structure is actually part of the ventilation system to the uranium mine tunnels in the area.

Take the very steep and rough road up the hillside past the ventilator and around the mountain. You may make it up this hill with a pickup, but four-wheel drive will keep your knuckles from turning white. Stay on this road for 1.6 miles, keeping left at the two forks. Park anywhere, and hunt on the hillsides all over the area. There are other roads in this area; there was also an active mine down in the canyon in 2012. The ventilation system is used by this mine, and some of the roads are now private, so make sure you stay on main roads and watch for NO TRESPASSING signs.

## Rockhounding

There is a lot of agate available in this area and it is best to get away from the traveled roads. In 2012 when we were there, we traveled into the hills surrounding this area in hopes of finding coprolites and did find a few. We found mostly agate and filled a few bags.

# 25. Hansen Creek: Agate, Petrified Wood

There are really nice pieces of wood to be found at the bottom of this canyon.

(See map on page 81.)

**Land type:** Mountains

**Elevation:** 4,633 feet

**GPS:** N37 46.114' / W110 44.450'

**Best seasons:** Spring through fall

**Land manager:** BLM

**Materials:** Agate, petrified wood

**Tool:** Rock hammer

**Vehicle:** High-clearance

**Special attraction:** Lake Powell

**Accommodations:** Motels; private RV parking and camping in Hanksville; public RV parking and camping at Star Springs Campground

**Finding the site:** From the intersection of UT 24 and UT 95 in Hanksville, drive south on UT 95 for 26.2 miles to the junction with UT 276. Follow UT 276 south for 17.1 miles to the well-marked Star Springs turnoff. Go 3.4 miles on the Star Springs Road to a dirt road marked with a BLM sign on your left. Take this road for 1.9 miles, where you will come to a fork. Keep left at the fork and continue for another 2.5 miles to the Shootering Canyon turnoff on the left. From the turnoff, continue southwest for 2.5 miles to a dirt road going left. Follow this road

Agate can still be found in this area.

for 0.4 mile to a fork. Go right at the fork for about 1 mile. At this point there is a steep crossing. If you don't want to try it, park in the flat and walk over to the hills to the left. When I was there in 2012, the road was completely washed out through the gully; you had to go to the south and make your way back up the gully to get back on the road. We hunted the canyon to the north of the gully and found a few nice pieces of petrified wood and some agate. This area has been well picked over.

## Rockhounding

Hansen Creek is another old collecting site that has been well picked over. There is still a lot of colorful agate here, but most of it is rather small. If you tumble stones, though, you will want to visit the site. You will end up with some really beautiful baroque stones that you can display with pride. A little careful searching will turn up some cabochon-size stones too.

On the way out you might want to try the left fork. It climbs to the top of the hills and just might lead to even more treasures.

Campsite by Star Springs for sites 24 and 25

# 26. Fry Canyon: Petrified Wood

Arch at top of the road in Fry Canyon

**Land type:** Mountains
**Elevation:** 5,580 feet
**GPS:** N37 34.870' / W110 7.103'
**Best seasons:** Spring and fall
**Land manager:** BLM
**Material:** Petrified wood
**Tool:** Rock hammer
**Vehicle:** Any
**Special attractions:** Lake Powell; Natural Bridges National Monument
**Accommodations:** Motel at Hite Marina; private RV parking at Fry Canyon Store
**Finding the site:** From the intersection of UT 95 and UT 276, drive south on UT 95 for 45.5 miles to the Fry Canyon Store. Don't expect this to be open. Take the unmarked dirt road at the left side of the store west for 4.4 miles. You will cross a small wash running north and south. Park off the road, and walk southward down

the wash. You will find some pieces of silicified wood along the wash, but in a hundred yards or so, you will come to a larger wash running east and west where you will find some much nicer pieces.

There are a lot of places in this area for petrified wood such as this.

When you have cleaned out the wash, you can continue on up the road for another 3.2 miles. This stretch is a little rough for the family car. A high-clearance vehicle would be much better. You will twist and turn up the mountain for a couple of miles. At 3.2 miles from the wash, you will see a sign for WEST MOSS BACK ROAD on the left. Take it for 0.2 mile, where there is a dirt road on the left (GPS: N37 35.191' / W110 08.841' or so); park off the road. The flats on both sides of the road have very nice specimens of silicified wood.

Picking up wood in Fry Canyon

# Site 26

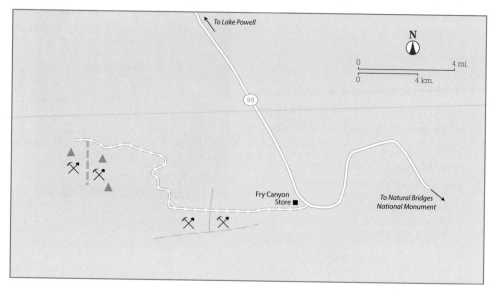

## Rockhounding

The Fry Canyon area is noted for petrified wood, and it is easy to find. The two sites listed above will help you to see what is in the area, but you should try as many of the roads and hike as far as you have time for. There are thousand of acres out here, and many have wood on them somewhere. This area is a long way from nowhere but well worth the trip, as the petrified wood is excellent and has some nice crystals attached. There is a gas station at Hite Marina, which you pass on the way to Fry Canyon, if you are running short.

# EAST UTAH

# 27. San Rafael: Agate, Jasper

Looking for jasper

**Land type:** High desert
**Elevation:** 4,156 feet
**GPS:** N38 50.265' / W109 58.487'
**Best seasons:** Spring and fall
**Land manager:** BLM
**Materials:** Agate, jasper, jasper conglomerate
**Tool:** Rock hammer
**Vehicle:** Any
**Special attractions:** Green River State Park and Museum
**Accommodations:** Motels; public and private RV parking and camping in Green River
**Finding the site:** From Green River, drive west on I-70 for 11 miles to exit 149. Go south on UT 24 for 0.6 mile to a dirt road leading west. Drive in for 0.2 mile or so, and park anywhere. If you go through the gate, there is a large turnaround.

# Site 27

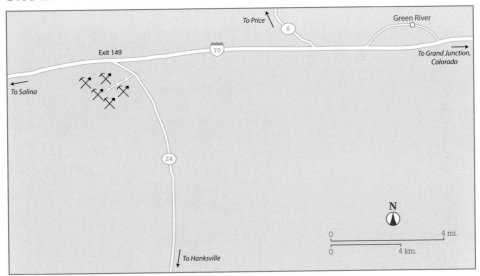

## Rockhounding

Hunt around in the low hills and flats on both sides of the road. There are some nice pieces of jasper and agate scattered about. You will see a lot of conglomerate made up of tiny pieces of jasper. If you find some good solid ones, they will make attractive cabochons. This is a good place to stop with the kids, since it is not far off the road. There is plenty of material for the tumbler. Search on nearby hills.

Road up to site; plenty of parking on top of the hill

# 28. Ruby Ranch Road 1: Agate

This road leads into the Ruby Ranch site 1.

**Land types:** High desert, hills
**Elevation:** 4,555 feet
**GPS:** N38 44.247' / W109 43.949'
**Best seasons:** Spring and fall
**Land manager:** BLM
**Material:** Agate
**Tool:** Rock hammer
**Vehicle:** Any
**Special attractions:** Green River State Park and Museum
**Accommodations:** Motels; public and private RV parking and camping in Green River
**Finding the site:** From Green River, go east on I-70 for 12.5 miles to exit 175 (mile marker 175). Drive south on the dirt Ruby Ranch Road for 5.5 miles to a dirt road to the left. Follow this road for 0.5 mile. When we visited this site, there was a steep

## Sites 28–30

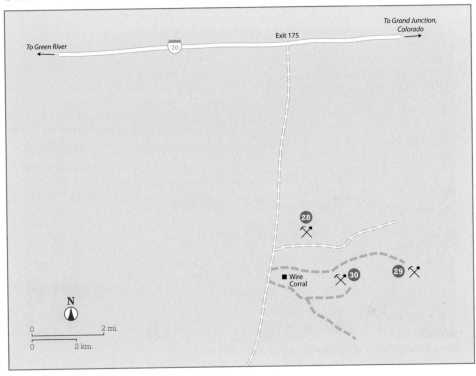

dip at 0.3 mile, which should make cautious drivers park the family car and walk the last 0.2 mile. No matter how you get there, at 0.5 mile begin your hunt.

### Rockhounding

There are several flats on the north where some nice agate can be found. This is not as productive as the other sites along Ruby Ranch Road, but it is one that can be reached in the family car.

# 29. Ruby Ranch Road 2: Agate

The road on the north side of the fenced corral leads into this area.

(See map on page 91.)

**Land types:** High desert, hills

**Elevation:** 4,540 feet

**GPS:** N38 50.922' / W109 58.921'

**Best seasons:** Spring and fall

**Land manager:** BLM

**Material:** Agate

**Tool:** Rock hammer

**Vehicle:** Four-wheel-drive

**Special attractions:** None

**Accommodations:** Motels; public and private RV parking and camping in Green River

**Finding the site:** From Green River, go east on I-70 for 12.5 miles to exit 175 (mile marker 175). Drive south on the dirt Ruby Ranch Road for 5.8 miles. At this point

At this site you will find green olive agate.

there is a large flat area to park. On the east side of the flat, you will see an old wire corral. Head toward the corral and take the dirt track that goes around to the left. Follow this for 1 mile. As you get behind the corral, you will cross a wash and then start up the hills. Beyond here the road gets very rough. Park and walk to the northeast. In a few yards you will top a little ridge and see acres and acres of agate.

## Rockhounding

The whole hillside, all the way up to the edge of the cliff, is covered with agate. Do a little walking, be patient, and you will find your treasure. Look carefully for big pieces peeking up through the grass. You can find green olive agate in this area. It is a red agate with small green, olive-like circles. These are not easy to find, but they are worth the time you spent looking for them.

# 30. Ruby Ranch Road 3: Agate

This hill contains some nice red and blue agates.

(See map on page 91.)
**Land types:** High desert, hills
**Elevation:** 4,452 feet
**GPS:** N38 50.340' / W109 58.399'
**Best seasons:** Spring and fall
**Land manager:** BLM
**Material:** Agate
**Tool:** Rock hammer
**Vehicle:** Four-wheel-drive
**Special attractions:** None
**Accommodations:** Motels; public and private RV parking and camping in Green River. You can also camp around the corral here; there is a big open flat for trailers and tents.

**Finding the site:** From Green River, go east on I-70 for 12.5 miles to exit 175 (mile marker 175). Drive south on the dirt Ruby Ranch Road for 5.8 miles. At this point there is a large flat area to park. On the east side of the flat, you will see an old wire corral. Take the track that goes to the right around the corral and drive 0.5 mile to a fork. At the fork, which is at the base of a small cliff, go left for another 0.5 mile. You will be roughly at the foot of the cliffs in Ruby Ranch Road 2 (site 29). There is a canyon just to the east of this site where you can also find good pieces of agate; you also might find some gastroliths in this area.

## Rockhounding

The agate here is much the same as at site 29. There is a lot of it over a very large area, so take your time and take home the best. This area is known for pigeon blood agate. It is a red agate with tiny dots of a darker red. On the way back you might want to give the right fork a try. Just beyond the turnoff as you go on the right fork, a road goes up to the top of a large hill. Agate can be found in this area also. This country is peppered with agate, so don't be shy about finding your own site.

More good agates can be found in this hill.

# 31. Yellow Cat Flat: Agate

Flat-topped butte to watch for

**Land types:** High desert, hills
**Elevation:** 4,384 feet
**GPS:** N38 39.790' / W109 50.300'
**Best seasons:** Spring and fall
**Land manager:** BLM
**Material:** Agate
**Tool:** Rock hammer
**Vehicle:** High-clearance
**Special attractions:** None
**Accommodations:** Motels; public and private RV parking and camping in Green River
**Finding the site:** From Green River, drive east on I-70 for about 30 miles to exit 193. Go south on the dirt road (Yellow Cat Road) for 5.8 miles. You will start up a hill; just at the top, turn right on the dirt track and drive 4.9 miles to a fork. Take

## Sites 31–35

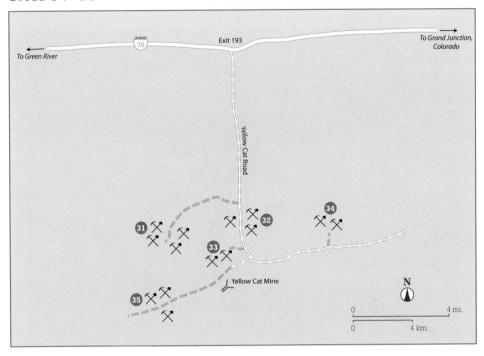

the right fork. In a little over 0.1 mile, you can park on the flat near a large flat-topped butte on your left. This is a good place to start your hunt. Make sure you have plenty of water and snacks; this area has very few sightseers, so you are on your own out here.

### Rockhounding

We found quite a bit of nice red agate on the flats to the right of the road. This is a huge area, and you will have to spend some time and walk all over it to find the best stuff. I don't really know if this is truly Yellow Cat Flat or not. I had conflicting maps and directions, and some said it was and others said it wasn't. I guess it doesn't matter much as long as you find some nice material. Don't be afraid to roam around; try any tracks going off in any direction. You never know what might be waiting to be discovered.

# 32. Yellow Cat Road: Agate

The farther you go from the road the better the agate in this area.

(See map on page 97.)

**Land type:** High desert

**Elevation:** 4,395 feet

**GPS:** N38 46.148' / W109 42.668'

**Best seasons:** Spring and fall

**Land manager:** BLM

**Material:** Agate

**Tool:** Rock hammer

**Vehicle:** Any

**Special attractions:** None

**Accommodations:** Motels; public and private RV parking and camping in Green River

**Finding the site:** From Green River, drive east on I-70 for about 30 miles to exit 193. Go south on the dirt road (Yellow Cat Road) for 7.2 miles. At this point the

In this area you can find agate and small amounts of barite crystals.

road drops down a little hill. At the bottom of the hill, park off the road and look on both sides for agate.

## Rockhounding

The flats and hills on both sides of the road contain agate. You can roam all over this area and find agate. The rule about getting away from the parking area works here. If there is a lot of agate near the road, there is a really good chance there will be even better pickings in the hills on both sides of the road. Give it a try. If you find an agate too big to lift by yourself, give me a call.

# 33. Yellow Cat Fork: Agatized Barite

Cutting these will make interesting barite cabs and display pieces.

(See map on page 97.)

**Land types:** High desert, hills

**Elevation:** 4,377 feet at the parking spot

**GPS:** N38 50.856' / W109 32.352'

**Best seasons:** Spring and fall

**Land manager:** BLM

**Materials:** Agate, agatized barite nodules

**Tool:** Rock hammer

**Vehicle:** Any

**Special attractions:** None

**Accommodations:** Motels; public and private RV parking and camping in Green River

**Finding the site:** From Green River, drive east on I-70 for about 30 miles to exit 193. Go south on the dirt road (Yellow Cat Road) for 7.9 miles. Just before you reach a fork, you will see a huge old tire from some sort of road machinery. It sits on the right-hand side of the road next to a dirt track heading west.

Drive along the track as far as you can, and park. Your destination is up the mountain to the west. If you have a high-clearance vehicle, you can drive most of the way. But unless a couple of washouts have been repaired since we were there, you will need four-wheel drive to go all the way.

## Rockhounding

Walk along the track as it climbs the hills. There is agate all along the way on both sides. You will find some of the agatized barite nodules along the way. They are coal black with red agate centers. Most occur as individual nodules, but some are in clusters like bunches of grapes. Nearly all will show a red-and-white agate center when cut. In some cases the red agate has replaced the barite needles. When these are cut, they show a fan of red needles against the black matrix and are very pretty. When we were looking, there were more barite nodules on the flats than up on the mountain. We followed the road to the top and found agate there but not many barite nodules, so it depends on what you are looking for at this site. This site has been picked over, but there are still some good specimens available.

# 34. Poison Strip: Agatized Barite

This road leads to Poison Strip.

(See map on page 97.)

**Land types:** High desert, hills

**Elevation:** 4,692 feet

**GPS:** N38 50.159' / W109 30.017'

**Best seasons:** Spring and fall

**Land manager:** BLM

**Material:** Agatized barite

**Tool:** Rock hammer

**Vehicle:** High-clearance

**Special attractions:** None

**Accommodations:** Motels; public and private RV parking and camping in Green River

**Finding the site:** From Green River, drive east on I-70 for about 30 miles to exit 193. Go south on the dirt road (Yellow Cat Road) for 7.9 miles. Just before you reach a fork, you will see a huge old tire from some sort of road machinery. It sits

Barite is hunted and found on this ledge.

on the right-hand side of the road next to a dirt track heading west. Just beyond this track, take the next fork to the east (Road 165) for 3.2 miles along the Poison Strip Road. At the bottom of the hill, a very rough track goes left for 0.4 mile to a flat. You might make it to the flat with a high-clearance vehicle, but four-wheel drive would make your life a lot easier. It is an easy walk, though, so one way or another, you can make it. This site has also been picked over, but we did find some material out on the flats around the GPS reading.

## Rockhounding

Whether you drive or walk to the flat, when you get there you will see some black and red agatized barite. Much of the material at this site is broken, but a little looking will turn up whole nodules and some of the "grape clusters" too. This is another good site for wandering around to see what else might be hiding. If you are part mountain goat, you just might turn up some really nice agate.

In case you were wondering, the Poison Strip got its name from some seeps that were contaminated with arsenic. This, coupled with the number of old uranium mines in the area, should tell you something about not licking the rocks.

# 35. Yellow Cat Mine Road: Agatized Barite

The barite balls are located on the flats beyond the mine.

(See map on page 97.)

**Land types:** High desert, hills

**Elevation:** 4,560 feet

**GPS:** N38 49.994' / W109 33.505'

**Best seasons:** Spring and fall

**Land manager:** BLM

**Material:** Agatized barite

**Tool:** Rock hammer

**Vehicle:** High-clearance

**Special attractions:** None

**Accommodations:** Motels; public and private RV parking and camping in Green River

**Finding the site:** From Green River, drive east on I-70 for about 30 miles to exit 193. Go south on the dirt road (Yellow Cat Road) for 7.9 miles. Just before you reach a fork, you will see a huge old tire from some sort of road machinery. It sits on the right-hand side of the road next to a dirt track heading west. Just beyond this track, take the right branch at the next fork. There are a few roads off from this one; just stay to the right. At just under 1 mile, you will pass an old uranium mine, which may be the Yellow Cat Mine. When you have gone 1.9 miles from the fork, you will come to a road going off to the right. Keep straight ahead. At 2.6 miles from the fork, you will come to a large flat where you can park and start hunting. This area is also picked over, but we did find some nice clusters where we parked.

## Rockhounding

There are black and red barite nodules all over the flats. It will take a little searching to find the best, but there are plenty here. There are also some of the nice "grape clusters."

Don't forget to watch along the road everywhere you go in this country. It is a vast area, and there are delights for the rockhound almost everywhere. It is also a long way from a bus stop; take plenty of water and snacks, and don't forget your emergency gear.

# 36. Bartlett Flat: Agate

The road out to Bartlett Flat

**Land types:** High desert, hills
**Elevation:** 5,183 feet
**GPS:** N38 23.432' / W109 27.263'
**Best seasons:** Spring and fall
**Land manager:** BLM
**Material:** Agate
**Tool:** Rock hammer
**Vehicle:** Any
**Special attractions:** None
**Accommodations:** Motels; public and private RV parking and camping in Green River and Grand Junction, Colorado
**Finding the site:** From Green River, drive east on I-70 for about 22 miles to Crescent Junction (exit 180). Go south on US 191 for another 20 miles to the intersection with UT 313. Follow UT 313 west for 8.5 miles to a dirt road going

# Site 36

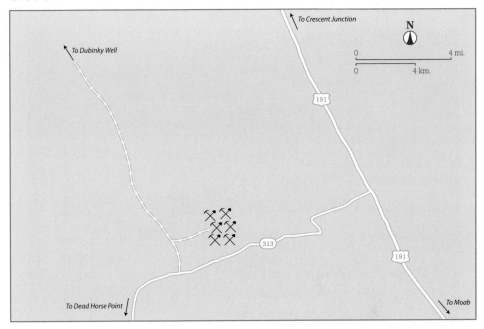

north. This is the Old Deadhorse Point Road. Follow this road for 1.5 miles to another unmarked road going east. Travel another 1.5 miles on this road to the top of a low hill. This area is now a nice camping area for trailers and tents.

## Rockhounding

The area on both sides of the road is covered with large patches of agate. They are not boulders, but there are plenty of pieces large enough for 30-by-40-millimeter cabochons. Roam around, and pick up the best pieces. Remember, the farther you get from the parking spot, the greater your chances for trophy winners.

According to my map, the road continues on to Dubinky Well. The wells were made during the Depression by youths who needed jobs. The youths were fed and clothed and were paid $30 per month, of which $25 was sent home. There is agate around the area by the wells; this is a place that you might want to visit.

# 37. Muleshoe Canyon: Agate

After a short drive you'll come to this gully.

**Land types:** High desert, hills
**Elevation:** 5,819 feet
**GPS:** N38 50.953' / W109 25. 708'
**Best seasons:** Spring and fall
**Land manager:** BLM
**Material:** Agate
**Tool:** Rock hammer
**Vehicle:** High-clearance
**Special attractions:** Arches and Canyonlands National Parks
**Accommodations:** Motels; public and private RV parking and camping in Moab
**Finding the site:** From the Old Spanish Trail Rodeo Arena at the south end of Moab, drive south on US 191 for 15.5 miles. At this point you will see the Northwest Pipeline Company buildings on your right. Continue for 0.6 mile; take the unmarked dirt road going left. Proceed for another 0.6 mile; take the dirt track

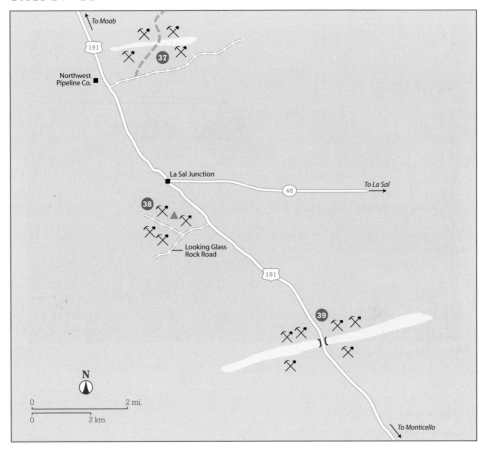

to the left. From this point on you will need a high-clearance or four-wheel-drive vehicle. It is about 0.5 mile on this track to the wash where you will start hunting. On your way, be sure to stop at Hole in the Rock—a home that was built inside a mountain and has an interesting history.

## Rockhounding

Agate is found over a large area in and around the wash. Most of it is white or clear, but with a lot of effort and walking, you should be able to find some nice colored pieces.

# 38. Looking Glass Road: Agate

Agate is all over in this area at the top of the hill.

(See map on page 109.)

**Land types:** High desert, hills

**Elevation:** 5,927 feet

**GPS:** N38 17.578' / W109 24.415'

**Best seasons:** Spring and fall

**Land manager:** BLM

**Material:** Agate

**Tool:** Rock hammer

**Vehicle:** Any

**Special attraction:** Looking Glass Rock

**Accommodations:** Motels; public and private RV parking and camping in Moab

**Finding the site:** From La Sal Junction south of Moab, drive south on US 191 for 0.7 mile to the intersection with Looking Glass Road. Turn right onto Looking Glass Road and proceed for another 0.7 mile to a dirt road on the right. Go through the

Samples of agate laying on this hill

gate and follow the dirt road for about 0.6 mile to the top of a little hill. Park off the road.

## Rockhounding

The areas on both sides of the road have patches of agate. It will take a little looking to find colorful pieces, but what's new about that?

Before you leave the area, be sure to proceed up Looking Glass Road to view Looking Glass Rock.

# 39. Joe Wilson Wash: Agate

Looking north and east up Joe Wilson Wash

(See map on page 109.)

**Land types:** High desert, wash, hills

**Elevation:** 5,736 feet

**GPS:** N38 15.309' / W109 22.885'

**Best seasons:** Spring and fall

**Land manager:** BLM

**Material:** Agate

**Tool:** Rock hammer

**Vehicle:** Any

**Special attraction:** Wilson Arch

**Accommodations:** Motels; public and private RV parking and camping in Moab

**Finding the site:** From La Sal Junction south of Moab, drive south on US 191 for 4.3 miles. You will cross the bridge over Joe Wilson Wash. Just beyond the bridge, there is a spot to the right where you can pull off and park. The bridge is now just

Wilson Arch on the way to Joe Wilson Wash

part of the road, with barriers down both sides, so don't expect to find an actual bridge to cross.

## Rockhounding

Cross the highway and walk back toward the bridge. From here you can work your way into the wash and the hills on both sides. There is a lot of territory to cover here, so try to spend some time searching.

If you didn't stop at the Wilson Arch on the way down, be sure to stop on the way back and enjoy this natural wonder. It is right off the highway, and there is a plaque with the history of the arch. If you haven't used up all of your energy rockhounding, hike up to the arch and take in the view.

There are some nice pieces of agate along the dry creek bed.

# NORTH UTAH

# 40. Sardine Summit:
## Fossils, Black Horn Coral

**Land type:** Road cut
**Elevation:** 5,800 feet
**GPS:** N41 33.254' / W111 57.256'
**Best seasons:** Spring through fall
**Land manager:** Utah State Division of Highways
**Materials:** Fossils, black horn coral
**Tool:** Rock hammer
**Vehicle:** Any

## Site 40

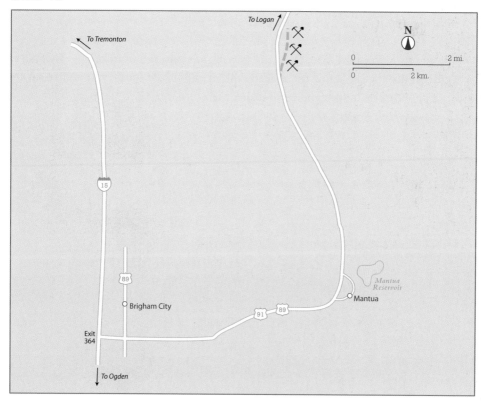

**Special attractions:** None

**Accommodations:** Motels; private RV parking and camping in Brigham City

**Finding the site:** From I-15, take exit 364 at Brigham City. Follow US 89/91 east for 10.3 miles to a huge road cut on the right. This cut is just over the summit and a short way past the highway maintenance sheds. This cut is now on state road property, and the UDOT (Utah Department of Transportation) will issue citations for parking along the road. When you get to the maintenance sheds, a short distance down the road on the east side is a gravel road that turns to the east. Pull off here, and park off the road. You can walk up the road or drive 0.1 mile to a large cut bank on the right.

## Rockhounding

This area has lots of fossil shells and some black horn coral. As you walk the road, look on the right side in the cuts that were made to put the road through; you will find fossils of different species just about everywhere. When you have your bucket full, you can proceed down to the cut in Sardine Canyon and look on the west side up by the top of the cut. We found a number of fossilized black horn coral specimens in this area; some are just lying there to be picked up. A word of warning: Be careful crossing the road—it is now a four-lane highway through here. There are barriers up through most of the canyon, so if you do not get across the road by the maintenance sheds, you will travel a couple of miles before you can make a turn to get back to them.

# 41. Riley's Canyon: Red Horn Coral

Some nice pieces of red horn coral can still be found at Riley's Canyon.

**Land type:** Mountains
**Elevation:** 7,853 feet
**GPS:** N40 34.097' / W111 11.628' (parking area GPS: N40 35.260' / W111 11.406')
**Best seasons:** Spring through fall
**Land manager:** Uinta National Forest
**Material:** Red horn coral
**Tools:** Rock hammer, small digging tools
**Vehicle:** Any
**Special attractions:** None
**Accommodations:** Motels in Park City and Heber; private RV parking in Park City; public and private RV parking and camping in Heber; national forest camping in the Kamas area
**Finding the site:** This site can be approached from several directions, so use any standard automobile map and get to the tiny town of Francis northeast of

# Site 41

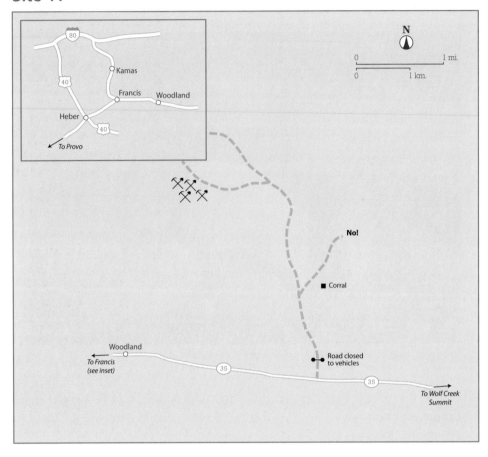

Heber and south of Kamas. From Francis, drive east on UT 35 to Woodland. At the Woodland Cash Store, check your odometer and drive 2 miles east. At this point you will see a pullout on the left side of the road. You will have to park here and hike to the site. The forest service closed the road several years ago to prevent further erosion and let the ground heal. The site is about 1.5 miles from the highway, but it is a pleasant walk with only a couple steep spots. It is fairly easy to follow the old road, but there is a fork at about 0.75 mile or so. You should go left, but the left track is faint. If you come to a fence around a deep hole on your right, you missed the fork. Backtrack and you will see it. As you come to the top of the ridge, you will see a track going left through some trees. Follow this and you will come out at the coral pit.

If you have an all-terrain vehicle (ATV), you can drive to the pit area on Cedar Hollow Road. Take Cedar Hollow Road up through the switchback and you will come to a fork in the road. Stay to the left; about 0.5 mile farther you will come to another fork. There are signs on the road; you will want to take Road 178. From here you will travel over two or three ridges approximately 2.5 miles, heading northwest, and come to another fork. Don't let this fool you. You will think you are going away from the pits, but the road is on a curve; you will come right back into the pits. The sign there says TO MOON SPRINGS. Take this road about 1 mile and you will come to the pits. The road is very rough and should only be used by ATVs. Go easy, and be safe. Use your helmets. If you want to try it, get in touch with the Uinta National Forest office in Kamas, Utah, for details.

## Rockhounding

This pit area has been dug in for many years, and it is not easy to find good specimens of red horn coral. You do have to dig into the many pits that are in the area to find material. Look for pieces that look like a horn in the white overburden in the area. When polished up, they make great specimens for the collector, but they're getting rare and hard to find, so good luck with your hunt. When I was there in 2012, we did find some small pieces of coral and one or two fairly good pieces.

# 42. Ophir: Pyrite

Galena ore can still be found along with pyrite.

**Land type:** Canyon
**Elevation:** 6,327 feet
**GPS:** N40 22.108' / W112 15.553'
**Best seasons:** Spring through fall
**Land manager:** Private
**Material:** Pyrite
**Tool:** Rock hammer (optional)
**Vehicle:** Any
**Special attractions:** None
**Accommodations:** Motels; limited public RV parking and camping at Tooele
**Finding the site:** From the intersection of Second Avenue North and Main Street in Tooele, drive south on UT 36 for 12.1 miles to the intersection with UT 73. Go east on UT 73 for 4.6 miles to the well-marked Ophir turnoff on the left. Follow this road for a little over 3 miles to the town of Ophir.

# Site 42

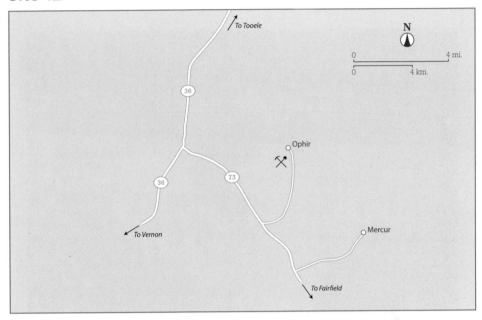

## Rockhounding

The large tailings pile you pass on the edge of town, the one that looks as though it has been scooped out, is the most prolific for pyrite. Virtually every rock in the pile has pyrite in it. We found peacock, malachite-coated rocks with pyrite, pyrite in quartz, and a host of others. This is all private land, and more and more people are moving in, so be sure to check locally (the little store is a good place to start) to see where collecting is okay. This is a great place to introduce kids to rockhounding; it is impossible not to find something.

Be sure to walk around Ophir. It is an old mining town with many mining artifacts and buildings from the 1800s. If you happen to be in Ophir in summer, check out the date of the Ophir Days celebration, usually held on a Saturday in late July or early August.

# 43. Tintic Mines: Minerals

The Tintic Mines area offers minerals such as chrysocolla, pyrite, and galena.

**Land type:** Mountains
**Elevation:** 6,400 feet
**GPS:** N39 54.616' / W112 7.982'
**Best seasons:** Spring through fall
**Land manager:** BLM, private claims
**Materials:** Mineral specimens
**Tool:** Rock hammer
**Vehicle:** Any (high-clearance or four-wheel-drive to some sites)
**Special attractions:** Historic Old Tintic Mining District; Mining Museum in Eureka
**Accommodations:** Motels; public and private RV parking and camping in Eureka area
**Finding the site:** Take US 6 west from I-15 to the town of Eureka, and take a look at the mountainsides. They are pockmarked with mines and tailings piles. Many are posted and some are still being worked, but there are so many that they are

# Site 43

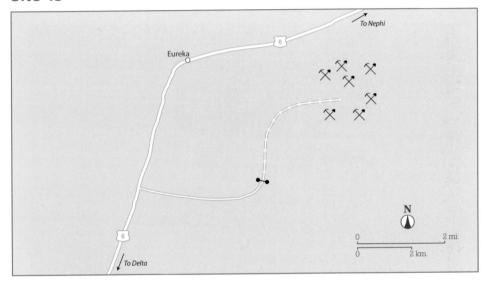

either on BLM land or are not posted that you will have no trouble finding places to hunt. If you make some local inquiries, you may be able to gain access to some of the posted mines as well. The map provided here will get you to one of the best collecting areas and will give you a good place to start.

To get to this site, go west from Eureka for about 2.5 miles to the well-marked road to Silver City. Follow this road for about 2 miles to where the pavement ends. Keep to the left on this road until you come to a flat where the road gets rougher and starts up the hill. When we were there in summer 2010, the road was closed to vehicle traffic, but this is a good place to park and hike through the old tailings up the road. It is not a difficult hike, and you will find more material while walking than you will just looking out the car window.

## Rockhounding

Many beautiful mineral specimens have been found in this area, but as usual with mine dumps and tailings piles, a lot of looking and poking around is necessary to find something worthwhile. Among the minerals that have been found here are quartz crystals, pseudomorphs of limonite after pyrite, malachite, azurite, galena, and many others. Search carefully; if you don't find anything in one place, move on to another. On a nice, cool fall day, you couldn't be in a better place for hunting.

# 44. Eureka: Agate

Around the old sites of Eureka, minerals of all kinds can be found.

**Land type:** Mountains
**Elevation:** 6,058 feet
**GPS:** N41 35.525' / W112 02.699'
**Best seasons:** Spring through fall
**Land manager:** BLM
**Material:** Agate
**Tool:** Rock hammer
**Vehicle:** High-clearance recommended
**Special attractions:** Historic Old Tintic Mining District; Mining Museum in Eureka
**Accommodations:** Motels; public and private RV parking and camping in Nephi area
**Finding the site:** From Tintic High School at the east end of Eureka, go east on US 6 for 3 miles. At this point an unmarked road goes north (left) toward the hills. Go through the gate (be sure to leave it as you find it) and proceed 0.7 mile.

# Site 44

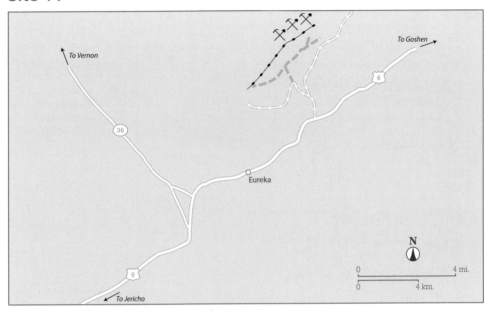

Here another unmarked road goes left. Follow it for 0.3 mile, where it makes a horseshoe turn to the left. Midway through the turn, a dirt track goes steeply up the hill ahead of you. Look at the top of the track and you will see a pole line. This is where you want to be. This road now has a NO TRESPASSING sign posted. You can walk (it's a little steep, but not far), or you can continue around the horseshoe and eventually end up at the pole line. There are a lot of side roads on this route, and driving there is quite a bit farther. My recommendation is to hike up the steep track.

No matter how you get there, when you reach the pole line, turn right and follow it for a hundred yards or so until it forks. Follow the left fork a short distance and you will see agate all over the ground and a virtual wall of agate to your left. This area has been thoroughly picked over since the first edition of this book. Not much remains here, but if you find agate, it makes some nice cabochons.

## Rockhounding

The agate here is mostly shades of tan and brown, but there are some pieces with nice reds in them. You have a choice of picking through the tons of material that have been dug out of the cliff wall or digging some out yourself.

I've done both, and aside from that feeling of being a hard-rock miner, I don't think there is any advantage to working so hard.

I said that spring and fall are the best times for hunting, but I opt for fall. There is a lot of scrub oak that turns the mountainsides bright red, and the brisk weather makes the short hike a real pleasure. No matter when you go, however, you will go home with agate.

*Caution:* If you explore much beyond this spot, be aware of private land. There are a number of posted spots. Don't be tempted to trespass.

# 45. Syringapora Mine: Syringapora

Syringapora pieces

**Land type:** Mountains
**Elevation:** 5,895 feet
**GPS:** N41 34.627' / W113 41.559'
**Best seasons:** Spring through fall
**Land manager:** BLM
**Material:** Syringapora chrysocolla
**Tools:** Rock hammer
**Vehicle:** Any
**Special attractions:** None
**Accommodations:** Camping on BLM land in this area
**Finding the site:** From the town of Snowville in northern Utah, take US 84 to exit 5, Park Valley. At the stop sign, turn left and follow UT 30 for 16 miles to the junction of UT 30 and UT 42. Turn on UT 30 and go 53 miles to mile marker 33. Turn right on a dirt road and follow this road for 2.2 miles where you will come to an old sign for the Immigrant Trail. Keep left and follow this road for 6.4 miles to where a

# Sites 45–46

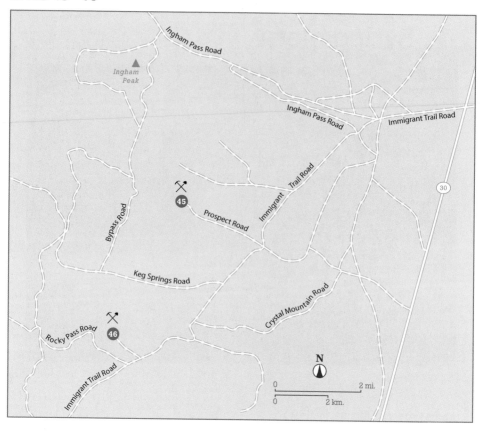

dirt road goes off to the right. Turn and follow this road for 2 miles into the mine area. At 2 miles there is a road that goes from this point up the hill. Follow this road for .3 mile and park. Look for an old Caterpillar parked under a tree.

## Rockhounding

This area is covered with mines and shafts; be careful. As you walk the area, you will see what looks like grey and white rock in a slag pile to the north and behind the old Cat. It doesn't look like much, but it will polish into very nice black and white cabochons for your treasure box. Other mines in the area have nice pieces of chrysocolla and some agate crystals have been taken from this area. *Caution:* Make sure that you stop in Snowville and fill your gas tank as there are no gas stations or restaurants in this area. The total round-trip to this site is just over 140 miles with no gas stations.

# 46. Garnet Mine: Garnet

Garnet material found at mine area

**Land type:** Mountains (See map on page 128.)
**Elevation:** 6,159 feet
**GPS:** N41 31.964' / W113 43.551'
**Best seasons:** Spring through fall
**Land manager:** BLM
**Material:** Garnet
**Tool:** Rock hammer (optional)
**Vehicle:** Any
**Special attractions:** None
**Accommodations:** Camping on BLM land in this area
**Finding the site:** From site 45, continue down the Immigrant Trail Road for 4.5 miles. Turn right and follow this not-so-traveled road to the end. You will see the small mine on your left.

## Rockhounding

This mine was once used to mine garnets to be crushed into sandpaper. These are not garnets that you would use for your nice jewelry. There are some nice small garnets to be found in the area, but you will need to dig for them as most of the surface area has been picked over. Just lately, on our trips to this mine, we have been coming up with small green crystals of peridot. This area has been burned off, so make sure that you have water with you when you go. There are no trees or shade in this area and the temperature can reach 100 degrees.

# CENTRAL UTAH

# 47. Birdseye: Birdseye Marble

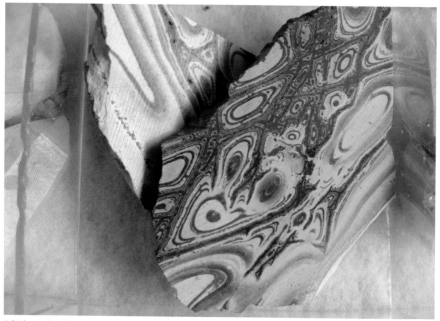

A little work with pick and shovel will give good results.

**Land type:** Mountains
**Elevation:** 5,342 feet at the gate (6,076 feet at meadow number 1)
**GPS:** N39 56.620' / W111 32.407' (N39 55.825' / W111 31.846' at meadow number 1)
**Best seasons:** Spring through fall
**Land manager:** Manti–La Sal National Forest
**Material:** Sedimentary
**Tools:** Rock hammer (heavy hammer, chisels, bars optional)
**Vehicle:** Four-wheel-drive
**Special attractions:** None
**Accommodations:** Motels; public and private RV parking and camping in Provo area
**Finding the site:** At the junction of US 6 and US 89, between Spanish Fork and Price, take US 89 south for 6.1 miles. At this point there is a dirt road to the left. At this writing there was also a red newspaper box at the edge of the highway.

# Site 47

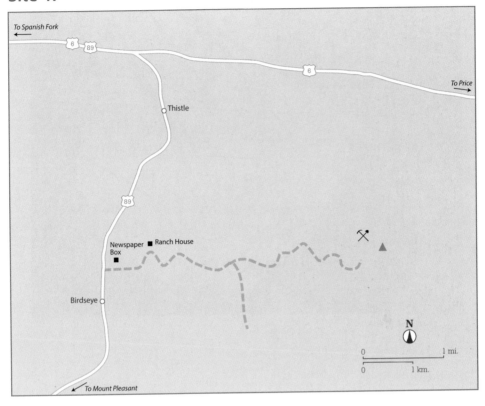

Turn onto the dirt road and pass through a gate. Be sure to leave the gate as you found it. Follow the road up the hill. At approximately 0.4 mile you will pass a ranch house on your left. Keep straight ahead. From this point on, the road gets increasingly more rugged; be prepared. At 1.5 miles from the gate, a fork goes right. Go straight and watch the sides of the road and gulleys to your left and pick up some fairly nice material. This road takes you to meadow number 1, where you can stop and find material up into the tree line on your left. The fence line in the trees mark the forest service boundary.

The quarry in this area is now all claimed and covers an area of 40 acres. Please be sure that as you are rockhounding in the area that you do not venture onto the claimed site, which is well marked; there are plenty of places to find birdseye other than the quarry.

Birdseye marble at site

## Rockhounding

The material found here is locally called birdseye marble. *Birdseye* for the circular patterning that resembles a bird's eye and *marble* because that's what they thought it was. The material is actually sedimentary stone, but does take a good polish. The little town of Birdseye got its name from this material.

# 48. Nephi: Petrified Palm

**Land type:** Cedar-covered hills
**Elevation:** 5,903 feet
**GPS:** N39 35.431' / W112 01.553'
**Best seasons:** Spring and fall
**Land manager:** BLM
**Material:** Petrified palm wood
**Tools:** Rock hammer, digging tools
**Vehicle:** Any to last 1.1 miles; four-wheel-drive beyond
**Special attractions:** None
**Accommodations:** Motels; public and private RV parking and camping in Nephi area
**Finding the site:** From exit 225 off I-15 in Nephi, take UT 132 west for 12.8 miles to an unmarked road to the left. This is the only road in the area; you will know you're

## Site 48

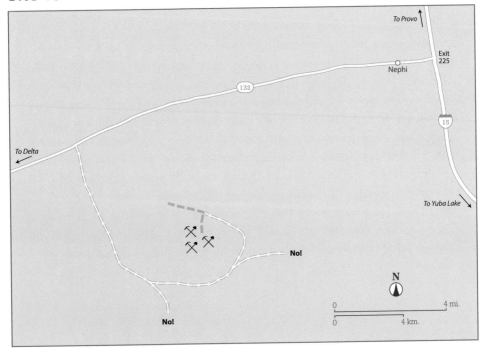

on the right track if you see an old gravel pit on the right at about 0.2 mile and cross a cattleguard at 0.3 mile. In about 1 mile, cross another cattleguard; at 4.5 miles you will reach a fork. Keep to the left, cross another cattleguard, see another fork, and keep to the right. At 7.4 miles you will come to another fork; keep to the left. At 9.9 miles you will see a small pump house ahead on the right. You can't miss it; it is the only structure out here. About 0.1 mile before you reach the pump house, a faint track goes up the hill to the left.

You could probably make the 1.1 miles to the site with a two-wheel-drive pickup, but four-wheel drive is best. If you are desperate for palm wood, you can walk it. No matter how you get there, you will know when you arrive. The area under the cedars has been "gopher holed" by hundreds if not thousands of rockhounds over the years.

## Rockhounding

This is one of those spots that will either make you the happiest rockhound in Utah or the most disgruntled. Some absolutely beautiful wood has been taken out of here over the years, but it is now very scarce. I've been out here and not found a chip, but in July 1995 I found some really nice small pieces, and Cora found three trophy winners. Two were about 3.5 inches in diameter and about as long, with beautiful bark definition on the outside and solid agate centers with great grain structure. Will you be as lucky? Who knows?

My untested theory is that although many have hunted here, there is still much to be dug. The key word is *dug*. You will notice that most of the holes are only a foot or so deep. If you want to test my theory, pick some holes and dig another foot or two. The soil is very sandy, and the digging is easy. Remember, though, that this theory is untested, so if you visit the site in mid-August and are digging away with sweat dripping off your nose and staining your sneakers and your rock bag is still empty, don't come looking for me. I warned you. On the other hand, you just might be within 2 inches of a full palm tree complete with fossilized fronds and coconuts. Should you keep digging? These are the decisions that make our hobby interesting. By the way, if you do go in August, be sure to take plenty of water and wear a hat—or you may see some of those coconuts. For summer, gnat spray is also a must.

# 49. Nephi: Calcite Onyx

What you're looking for can often be found where others have been digging.

**Land type:** Mountains

**Elevation:** 6,277 feet (at parking area); 6,521 feet (at site)

**GPS:** N39 45.881' / W111 42.494' (at parking area); N39 46.081' / W111 42.564' (at site)

**Best seasons:** Spring through fall

**Land manager:** Uinta National Forest

**Material:** Calcite onyx

**Tool:** Rock hammer

**Vehicle:** Any

**Special attraction:** Nebo Loop Road drive

**Accommodations:** Motels; public and private RV parking and camping in the Nephi area; national forest campground next to the site

**Finding the site:** From exit 225 off I-15 in Nephi, take UT 132 east for 4.8 miles to the Nebo Loop Road turnoff. Follow the Nebo Loop Road for about 3.5 miles, where a fork to the left goes to the Bear Canyon, Ponderosa Campground. Stay

# Site 49

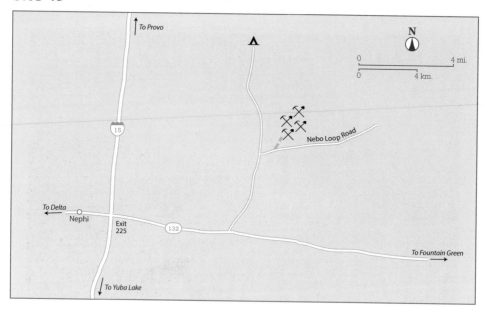

on the loop road for approximately 0.2 mile to a parking area on the left. You will have to keep a sharp eye out for this area. It is just a little flat down in the trees and is seldom used. If you miss the spot, it is quite a ways to a turnaround. When you are in the parking area, you can see the faint trail (actually an old road) heading up the hill on the other side of the little creek. Follow this trail to the onyx site. It took Cora and me about fifteen minutes to hike it. It may take you five minutes or five hours. Actually, the hike is not bad. It is a little steep in places, but there is a reasonable amount of shade on the way. We did it in mid-July; fall is better.

## Rockhounding

This is an old collecting site, but there are tons of material left. Like the wonderstone at Vernon (site 60), others have done a lot of the hard work, and you can find all the material you will ever need on the ground. If you like to bang walls with your hammer, don't let me stop you. It's a good way to take out your aggressions.

When you finish collecting, go over the Nebo Loop Road. It is a beautiful drive any time of year, but in the fall it is spectacular.

# 50. Yuba Lake: Birdseye Rhyolite

Be on the lookout for this parking lot beside the entrance to Yuba Lake.

**Land type:** Hills
**Elevation:** 5,046 feet
**GPS:** N39 24.468' / W112 1.793'
**Best seasons:** Spring and fall
**Land manager:** BLM
**Material:** Birdseye rhyolite
**Tool:** Rock hammer
**Vehicle:** Any
**Special attraction:** Yuba Lake State Park
**Accommodations:** Motels; public and private RV parking and camping in Nephi area
**Finding the site:** Leave I-15 at exit 202, and drive 1.5 miles toward Yuba Lake. You will see a road going down to the lake on the left and an OFF HIGHWAY VEHICLE AREA sign on the right. Park in the OHV area as far as you can toward the red hills ahead.

# Site 50

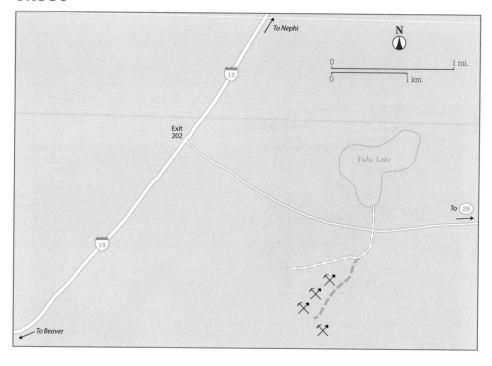

When you have gone as far as your vehicle will let you, park and hike around on the hills to find the rhyolite.

## Rockhounding

The material here is a birdseye rhyolite, but it is nothing like the beautiful material at the birdseye quarry (site 47). The matrix is a grayish color, and the eyes are gray with white bands inside. Some of the material can be cut to show the eyes and bands, which makes a nice display. The "eyes" have weathered out of much of the matrix and can be found all over the hills. They range in size from about 0.5 inch to nearly 2 inches. When they are cut in half, they show little bull's-eye rings. You may as well take a few home with you. They don't take up much space, and you may find that you are the only one on your block with such treasures.

# 51. Salina: Wonderstone

Some digging and luck will produce nice pieces for cabbing.

**Land type:** Mountains
**Elevation:** 6,837 feet
**GPS:** N38 53.860' / W111 48.219'
**Best seasons:** Spring through fall
**Land manager:** Fishlake National Forest
**Material:** Wonderstone
**Tool:** Rock hammer
**Vehicle:** Any
**Special attractions:** None
**Accommodations:** Motels; public and private RV parking and camping at Salina
**Finding the site:** From the intersection of US 50 and US 89 in Salina, drive east on Main Street for 0.2 mile to 300 East. Turn right onto 300 East and follow it to the tunnel under I-70. If you are pulling a trailer, you cannot take it under the tunnel; you will need to go back and take the Gooseberry exit off I-70 (exit 63). If you are coming

# Site 51

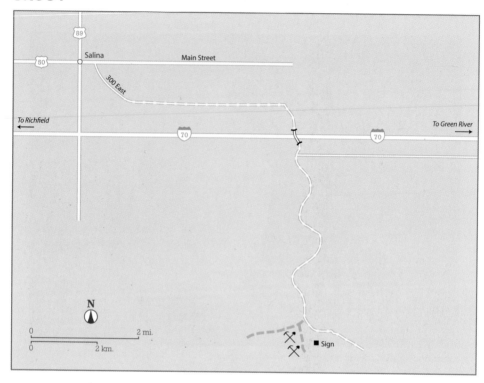

from Green River, take exit 63 and follow the dirt road west to the tunnel. From the tunnel, go south on the forest road up Soldier Canyon for 3.1 miles to a fork. A sign at the fork directs you to Mud Springs and a few other places. If you go about 0.3 mile up the right fork, you will see a ledge on your left where many a rockhound has dug wonderstone. There is a nice place to park here, and you can hunt along the ledge. If you have no luck, or you tire of the ledge, go back to the fork and try the left-hand road. Look for spots where others have dug, and give them a try.

## Rockhounding

The Salina Canyon wonderstone is harder and denser than that from the Vernon area (site 60). It has very nice bands, swirls, and eyes and makes nice cabochons. It does not take a high polish like agate but does have a very pretty satin sheen. You will find some nice little pieces around the ledges, but to get the best you will have to find a seam and work at it with bars, chisels, and heavy hammers. If you find a nice seam, the work required to free the stone will be worth it.

# 52. Last Chance Road: Agate

This is the site at the Last Chance Road.

**Land types:** High desert, hills
**Elevation:** 6,100 feet
**GPS:** N38 39.681' / W111 18.243'
**Best seasons:** Spring and fall
**Land manager:** BLM
**Materials:** Agate, barite nodules
**Tool:** Rock hammer
**Vehicle:** Any
**Special attractions:** None
**Accommodations:** Motels; public and private RV parking and camping in Green River and Salina
**Finding the site:** This site can be reached from either the Green River area or Salina. From Salina, drive approximately 34 miles east on I-70 to exit 91. From Green River, drive about 58 miles west on I-70 to the same exit. At exit 91 a dirt

# Site 52

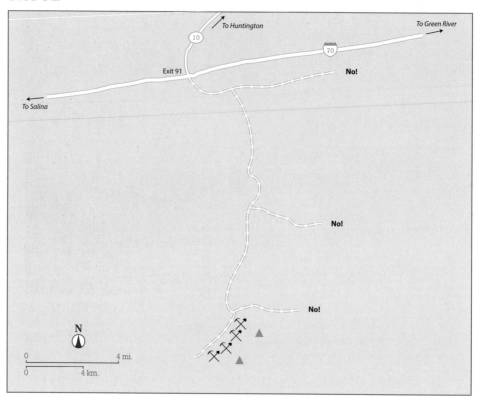

road curves to the east. Follow it for 2 miles. At this point another dirt road heads south. Follow this road for 5.4 miles to a fork. At the fork go right for another 3.8 miles to another fork. Go right again for just 0.4 mile. You will see a wide flat area on your left. You should be in the area of Willow Springs. Drive in, and park anywhere.

## Rockhounding

This is one of the most prolific sites in Utah. Looking south from the parking area, you will see a virtual ocean of agate. Nearly every rock you can see is agate, and in most places it is impossible to walk without stepping on this beautiful material. It can be found in a wide variety of colors, and although most pieces are small, it is easy to find some from which you can get several 30-by-40-millimeter cabochons.

Some of the best agate at this site is laying in the parking area just waiting to be collected.

As a bonus, there are also tons of little gray barite balls. They range from pea-size to golf ball–size and make nice cabinet specimens.

We didn't follow the agate trail over the saddle to the south, but if you have the time and the inclination, you might find some more or better material by walking a little farther.

# 53. Wendover: Agate

Follow the road as far up the mountain as you dare drive, and then start your hunt.

**Land type:** Mountains
**Elevation:** 4,913 feet
**GPS:** N40 49.923' / W113 57.665'
**Best seasons:** Spring and fall
**Land manager:** BLM
**Material:** Agate
**Tool:** Rock hammer
**Vehicle:** Any
**Special attractions:** Bonneville Speedway and Speed Museum
**Accommodations:** Motels; private RV parking in Wendover
**Finding the site:** Leave I-80 at exit 4 just east of Wendover. Go north to the truck stop next to the freeway. From here you will see a paved road heading toward the hills. This is the road to the Bonneville Speedway. Follow it for 1.1 miles to a gravel road to the left. Take the gravel road 0.7 mile to a fork. The right fork goes to the

# Site 53

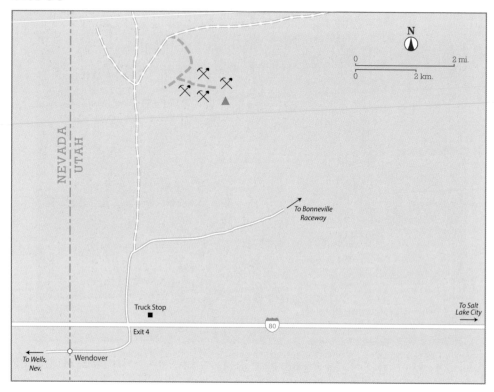

dump. Recheck your odometer, and take the left fork for about 2.4 miles. At this point, check your GPS and follow any of the roads that go off to the right of this main road. When you get close to the GPS reading, you can start looking for agate. The GPS reading is where a couple of roads come together, and we found agate to the west and east of this parking area. Finding this site is a lot easier than it sounds. Trust me!

## Rockhounding

Hunt all over the area where you are parked. The agate is widely scattered, smallish, and not terribly plentiful, but it has nice moss in it and is very pretty. Most pieces are big enough for cabochons for rings, small pendants, or stickpins.

If you entered Wendover from the east, you may have noticed a bunch of dilapidated buildings and a big rusty hanger at the southeast edge of town.

You'll see this sign on the way to the dig.

These are the remains of Wendover Air Force Base. In this remote spot the US Air Force trained bomber pilots during World War II. This is not really remarkable unless you know that the names of two of those bombers were *Enola Gay* and *Bock's Car*—the B-29s that dropped atomic bombs on Hiroshima and Nagasaki. All the top-secret training for those missions took place in this remote and barren spot. Three atomic bombs were assembled at Wendover for the missions. Little Boy, the Hiroshima bomb, did not have its nuclear components installed until it was in the Pacific. But two Fat Man bombs, one of which was dropped on Nagasaki, had their plutonium cores installed at the Wendover base.

# 54. Gold Hill: Azurite, Malachite

The old sign is still standing at Gold Hill.

**Land type:** Mountains
**Elevation:** 5,300 feet
**GPS:** N40 9.975' / W113 49.852'
**Best seasons:** Spring and fall
**Land manager:** BLM
**Materials:** Feldspar, malachite, azurite, quartz, aragonite, jasper
**Tool:** Rock hammer
**Vehicle:** Any
**Special attractions:** none
**Accommodations:** Motels; private RV parking in Wendover. Trailer parking is available in and around Gold Hill. Check with local residents for camping.
**Finding the site:** From West Wendover, Nevada, take ALT US 93 south toward Ely, Nevada. At 25.7 miles a sign points to a paved road to Ibapah, Gold Hill, and Partoun. Follow this road to the east for 16.5 miles. At this point another sign directs you to a gravel road to the left leading to Gold Hill. After 11.7 miles you

# Site 54

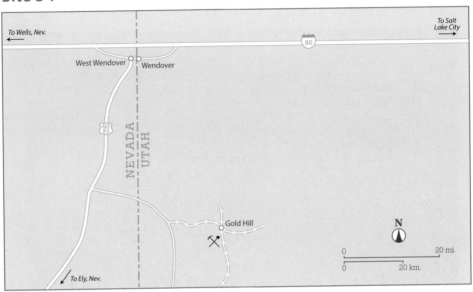

will enter the town of Gold Hill. Look around at the old buildings, read the BLM sign that tells a little of the town's history, and then go rockhounding. Make sure you start with a full tank of gas from Wendover—there is no gas available in Gold Hill.

## Rockhounding

The hills around Gold Hill are dot-ted with old mines, prospect holes, tailings piles, shafts, and drifts. This area is almost all BLM or state land, but there are spots of private property and active or patented claims. All the latter seem to be well posted, so unposted land should be fair game. If you can find anyone around town, you can check. We had the best luck with tailings right next to the road, within about 0.5 mile from town on the road going south toward Callao.

Material is still there for the finding at the old mine sites around Gold Hill.

# 55. Obsidian Hill: Apache Tears

Apache tears are all over the ground here.

**Land types:** High desert, hills
**Elevation:** 5,200 feet
**GPS:** N39 41.946' / W113 10.005'
**Best seasons:** Spring and fall
**Land manager:** BLM
**Material:** Apache tears
**Tools:** None
**Vehicle:** Any
**Special attractions:** None
**Accommodations:** Motels in Delta; tent and trailer camping in area
**Finding the site:** From the turnoff to Topaz Mountain on UT 174 (Brush Wellman Road), drive 6.2 miles west to the end of the pavement. At the end of the pavement, the road becomes a gravel road going straight ahead; another road goes to the left. To the right of the road and intersection, there is a small hill at

## Sites 55–56

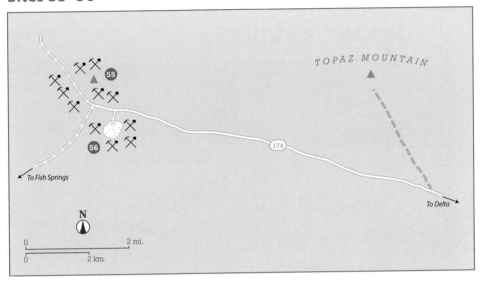

about a 45-degree angle, or two o'clock, to the left. This is the hill where you will find the Apache tears. The whole area off to the right has Apache tears and bigger pieces of obsidian.

## Rockhounding

This is a great place for the kids or for anyone who has the desire to collect some nice Apache tears. They are all over the place out here, but the best concentrations seem to be on top of the little hills.

# 56. Butterscotch Hill: Jasper Pebbles

Just off the side of the road, this pit contains jasper pebbles.

(See map on page 149.)
**Land types:** High desert, hills
**Elevation:** 5,200 feet
**GPS:** N39 41.653' / W113 10.139'
**Best seasons:** Spring and fall
**Land manager:** BLM
**Material:** Tumbled jasper pebbles
**Tools:** None
**Vehicle:** Any
**Special attractions:** None
**Accommodations:** Motels in Delta; tent and trailer camping in area
**Finding the site:** From the turnoff to Topaz Mountain on UT 174 (Brush Wellman Road), drive 6.2 miles west to the end of the pavement. At the end of pavement,

Jasper pebbles are not difficult to find here.

the road becomes a gravel road going straight ahead; another road goes to the left. Just before the end of the pavement, look at the hills on your left and you will see some diggings on the hillside. There is a track going to the diggings, and you can pull into the pit with no real problem. The diggings are only about 0.1 mile, though, so you can park off the road and walk to them easily.

## Rockhounding

We discovered this site entirely by accident. We were heading home from the Apache tears site and spotted a cut on the opposite side of the road. Of course we had to see what was there, so over we went. (One of the nice things about these kinds of discoveries is that you get to name them. Hence the name Butterscotch Hill.) Evidently someone had been looking for gravel at one time and dug a pit in the process. There is gravel all right, but a good share of it is made up of little jasper pebbles in shades of tan and brown that look like those butterscotch chips in cookies. There are also a few nicely figured pieces of agate. They all look as though they just came out of the tumbler after the final polish. My best guess is that this must have been a riverbed long ago. The pebbles are fun to collect if you are in the area, and the kids should have a great time too.

# 57. Topaz Mountain:
## Topaz, Beryl, Garnet

The hills in Topaz Basin

**Land type:** Desert, mountains
**Elevation:** 5,758 feet at the base
**GPS:** N39 41.781' / W113 5.878'
**Best seasons:** Spring and fall
**Land manager:** BLM
**Materials:** Topaz, beryl, garnet
**Tools:** Rock hammers, thin chisels, screwdrivers, screens
**Vehicle:** Any (high-clearance recommended)
**Special attractions:** None
**Accommodations:** Motels in Delta; tent and trailer camping at site
**Finding the site:** From the intersection of US 6 and US 50 on the eastern edge of Delta, take US 6 northeast for 10.3 miles to the junction with UT 174 (known locally as the Brush Wellman Road). Go northwest on Brush Wellman Road for 37.5

# Site 57

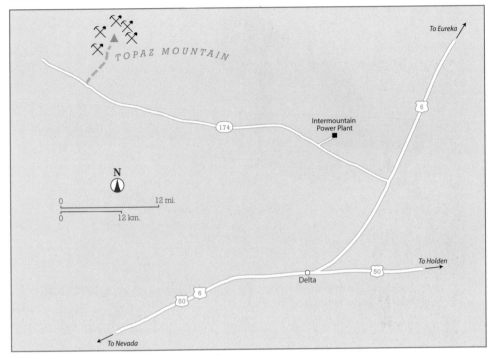

miles. A well-marked dirt road on the right goes a little over 2 miles to the area known as the "amphitheater" at Topaz Mountain.

## Rockhounding:

Although garnet, beryl, and a few other gemstones have been found at Topaz Mountain, the real prize is topaz. Specifically, the prize is the sherry-colored topaz, which is Utah's state gem. Finding one of these prizes, however, is not a matter of stepping out of the car and twisting your ankle on a ten-pound topaz. There is no doubt that some of the most beautiful topaz anywhere has been taken from this mountain. There is also little doubt that much beautiful topaz remains on the mountain. But it is a big mountain with a lot of hiding places for the wily topaz, and the mountain is not going to give up its treasures without making us work for them.

There are several ways to go about collecting here. The simplest way is just to look around for sparkles on the ground and follow them to see what you can find. Many small specimens are found in this way. Be sure and take a

A friend hunting for topaz in a sandy wash in Topaz Basin

screen, as I have found some really nice specimens by screening in the washes and at the base of the hills in this area. By screening for specimens, you can sometimes follow the washes up to where the topaz has broken off from the rock and find better sherry-colored ones there. This is kind of like looking for gold.

A second way to is to do a little hiking around the base of the mountain and look in the little washes and ravines where stones can become lodged behind rocks and debris in the runoff. The way to get the real beauties, however, is to work around the mountain, looking for the white rocks in the seams that contain topaz. Start where someone else has been working to get the feel for what needs to be done. Use your rock hammer, chisels, or even screwdrivers to probe for pockets in the seams. Open the pockets and hope for the best. The mountain is full of topaz. If you work long enough and hard enough, you will go home with a big smile and maybe some world-class topaz.

# 58. Drum Mountains: Agate

One of many pits in the Drum Mountains

**Land types:** High desert, hills
**Elevation:** 5,332 feet
**GPS:** N39 37.939' / W113 1.915'
**Best seasons:** Spring and fall
**Land manager:** BLM
**Material:** Agate
**Tools:** Rock hammer (heavy hammers and chisels optional), pick, shovel
**Vehicle:** Any
**Special attractions:** None
**Accommodations:** Motels in Delta; tent and trailer camping in area
**Finding the site:** From the intersection of US 6 and US 50 at the east end of Delta, take US 6 northeast toward Eureka for 10.3 miles to the junction of UT 174 (known locally as the Brush Wellman Road). Go left on this road and drive 35.2 miles to a dirt road to the left. The only problem with finding this road is that there are dirt

# Site 58

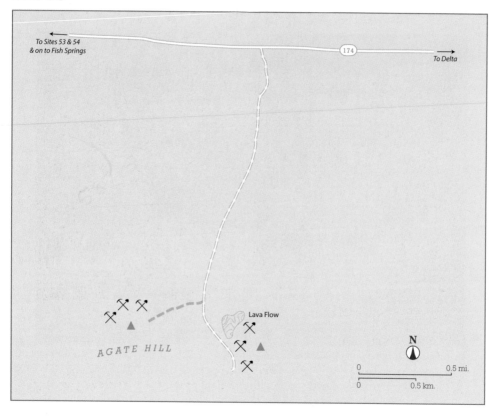

roads to the left at 31.3 miles and 33.4 miles. If your odometer and mine are good friends, you will be all right. The best bet is to ignore the first two roads you come to and take the third. It is the closest one to the large hill on your right. Go south for 1.3 miles and you will see a small black lava flow on the left side of the road. Just before you reach the flow, a faint track goes right toward "agate hill." Drive up this track for about 0.3 mile, and park in the wide flat area. Hike on the old road going up the hill, and prepare yourself for a great agate collecting experience. Be careful, as this hill seems to grow rattlesnakes. You will need to have a pick and shovel—there are some big pieces of agate here.

If you take the gravel road going south, you will come into the ghost town of Joy. There are mine tailings and pits to look around and explore. We missed Joy twice while trying to find it; all that remains are a couple of rock walls and a freshwater spring.

Looking out from the Drum Mountains

## Rockhounding

We looked for this site before with no luck. We got a lot of dirt-road driving practice, but the person who gave us the directions was evidently cartographically challenged. I am glad we persevered, however, because this turned out to be one of the premier collecting sites in the state. I am almost tempted to break my word to you and start raving about colors. You will have to be the judge, but I think you will like this spot. This takes a lot of digging and hard work, but you will get some of the best agate in the area.

If you get tired of agate hill, there is a little agate behind the lava flow and on the hill just southeast of it. This is not as good as agate from the hill, but it is easier to get.

You might also want to keep your ears open for deep booming sounds from below. The Drum Mountains got their name from such sounds coming from deep in the Earth. I don't know what causes such sounds, unless it is a bunch of new agate trying to find its way to the surface.

# 59. Dugway: Geodes

Dugway geode

**Land type:** Desert
**Elevation:** 4,833 feet
**GPS:** N39 53.622' / W113 8.205' (pit area)
**Best seasons:** Spring and fall
**Land manager:** BLM
**Material:** Geodes
**Tools:** Digging tools
**Vehicle:** High-clearance
**Special attractions:** Sights along the Simpson Springs–Callao Road
**Accommodations:** This is a very remote spot, and accommodations are generally pretty far away. There is open camping on the BLM land, but the closest motels and RV parks are in Delta or in the Tooele area.
**Finding the site:** There are two basic ways to reach the Dugway site. From the north or central part of the state, drive to Vernon, which is south of Tooele on UT

# Site 59

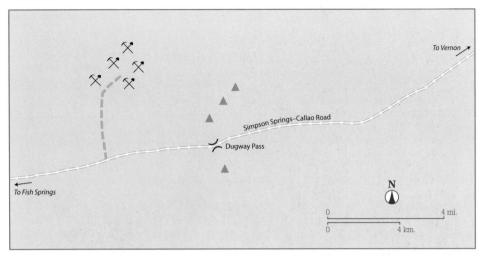

36. About 2 miles north of Vernon is the turnoff for the Simpson Springs–Callao Road. There is a roadside marker for the Pony Express. From the turnoff on UT 36, it is about 50 miles from Vernon to Dugway Pass. This is all gravel road and at times very washboard. At the pass, check your odometer and drive an additional 4 miles. At this point a dirt road goes to the right. There is a BLM sign to the geode beds. The best spot is said to be about 3 miles in, but there is a lot of territory to explore. Look for the very obvious signs of previous digging, and try them.

If you are in the area around Delta, you can drive north past Topaz Mountain (site 57) to Dugway Pass. This also is a good 50-mile trip, but the roads are usually unmarked and a little tricky to find. If you go out to the geode beds, make sure you have plenty of gas and good tires. I have helped change or reinflate a lot of flat tires in this area so that drivers could get back to Vernon.

## Rockhounding

This is one of the most famous of all the Utah rockhounding sites. Be fore-warned, however, that a lot of searching and serious digging will be required to find the trophy winners. On the other hand, many nice broken but pretty pieces have been picked up in and around the old diggings. The summers here are very hot and the winters very cold, but if you are persistent, you just may go down in the record books with a real find. There are claims in some areas, so make sure you check to see which claims are active and where you

Author digging for geodes in one of the many pits at Dugway

can dig for geodes. There are many areas where you can find geodes, so just look where others have been digging. Usually the geodes are found in or just under the clay level; if you find a nice pocket, you can get a lot of them in a short time.

Crystal skull geode

# 60. Vernon: Wonderstone

There are some nice pieces to be found with some digging.

**Land type:** Hills
**Elevation:** 5,669 feet
**GPS:** N40 6.145' / W112 21.434'
**Best seasons:** Spring through fall
**Land manager:** BLM
**Material:** Wonderstone
**Tools:** Rock hammer (heavy hammer and chisels optional)
**Vehicle:** Any (high-clearance recommended)
**Special attractions:** Historic Old Tintic Mining District; Mining Museum in Eureka
**Accommodations:** Motels; public and private RV parking and camping in Tooele and at site area
**Finding the site:** Drive south out of Vernon, which is south of Tooele, on UT 36 until you come to a set of railroad tracks; you will see an unmarked road to the left. There are some utility buildings by the side of the road there. Follow this

# Site 60

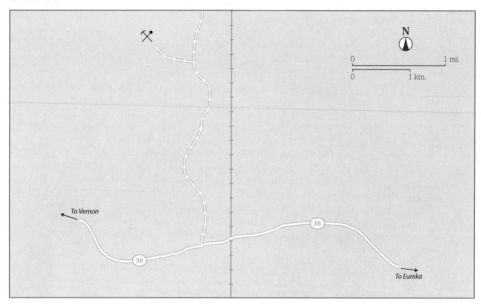

road, which parallels the tracks, for approximately 2 miles to a fork. Take the left fork toward the low hills. Almost immediately you will see the reddish color of the wonderstone pit. Drive up to it and park.

## Rockhounding

This is another site where you can't go wrong. There is much material lying on the ground just waiting for a good home. Your only problem will be which ones to adopt. You may choose to work on the wall of the pit for your prizes, but I can't imagine why anyone would want to work that hard when there is so much material just lying there. To each his or her own! I guess if someone hadn't done all that work before, you and I would have to now.

Wonderstone

# SOUTHWEST UTAH

# 61. Skull Rock Pass: Fossils

Park on the side of the road and look in the right-of-way for fossils.

**Land type:** Road cut
**Elevation:** 5,256 feet
**GPS:** N39 1.908' / W113 20.536'
**Best seasons:** Spring and fall
**Land manager:** Utah State Division of Highways
**Material:** Fossils
**Tools:** Rock hammer and shale-splitting tool
**Vehicle:** Any
**Special attractions:** None
**Accommodations:** Motels; private camping and RV parking in Delta
**Finding the site:** From the top of the viaduct on US 6 and US 50 at the west end of Delta, drive west on US 6/50 for 48.5 miles. At this point you will see the long road cut on both sides of the highway. Find a place where you can park safely off the road, and hunt all along the cut. This is all state road property, so make sure

# Site 61

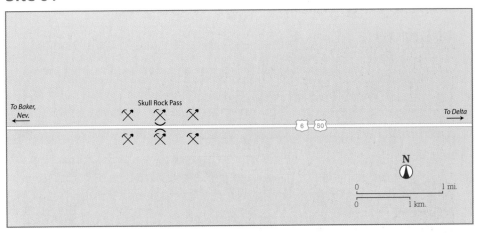

you watch for cars and big rigs traveling this road. When we were there in 2012, they were widening the road through this pass, and it was pretty much torn up. We looked and did find some fossils at this site.

## Rockhounding

The shale layers contain various Ordovician fossils, including some trilobites. The chances of finding trilobites like those at Antelope Spring (site 65) are slim, but there are bits and pieces in the layers. There are several spots where the shale layers are thin and easily separated with just a pocketknife blade and others where more persuasive measures must be used. There is a lot of shale to look over here, so take your time and look for the best specimens. When I was there in 2012, there was not really anything to write home about. If I were you, I would go on to the other sites in this area.

# 62. Conger Spring: Fossils

You'll find these old concrete foundations at Conger Spring.

**Land type:** High desert
**Elevation:** 6,672 feet
**GPS:** N39 11.390' / W113 43.446'
**Best seasons:** Spring and fall
**Land manager:** BLM
**Material:** Fossils
**Tools:** Rock hammer, trowel, screen
**Vehicle:** Any
**Special attractions:** None
**Accommodations:** Motels; private RV parking and camping in Delta
**Finding the site:** From the top of the viaduct on US 6 and US 50 at the west end of Delta, drive west on US 6/50 for 72.5 miles to milepost 16. At this point a BLM sign directs you to turn right toward Little Valley. At 1.3 miles from the highway, a road goes left to Little Valley Well; keep straight ahead. At 3.9 miles from

# Site 62

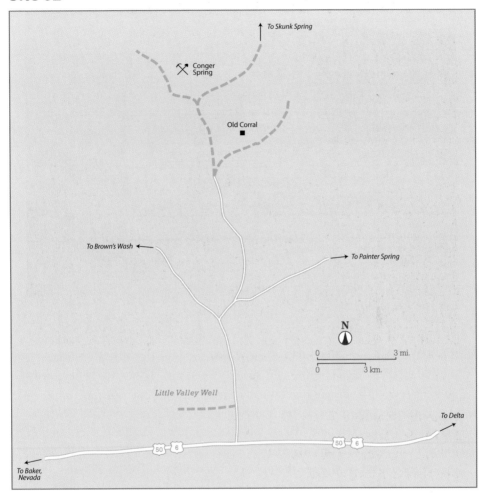

To Skunk Spring

Conger Spring

Old Corral

To Brown's Wash

To Painter Spring

N

| 0 | 3 mi. |
| 0 | 3 km. |

Little Valley Well

To Delta

50 6

50 6

To Baker, Nevada

the highway, you will come to a fork; keep right. At 4.4 miles you will come to another fork; keep left. At 9.6 miles you will come to a third fork; keep left. At 11.9 miles there is yet another fork; keep left again. At 13.1 miles you will see the old concrete foundations of Conger Spring on your right. Pull in, and park near the foundations and the old watering trough.

## Rockhounding

To the east of the concrete foundations, you will see where digging has taken place in the banks and along the washes. You will find crinoids, horn coral, and

Go up this draw to find fossils.

brachiopods all over this area. Just stoop over and pick them up. Your toughest job here will be deciding the best specimens to take home. Of course, as in most places, a little digging will usually turn up even better specimens.

This spot is a long way from anywhere. In fact, the stretch of US 6/50 between Delta, Utah, and Baker, Nevada, is known locally as the loneliest highway in America. But if you are a fossil hound, you will forget all about the long drive when you see the objects of your search. The coral here is estimated to be over sixty million years old, so you had better get out there and pick some up soon. It may not wait for you much longer.

# 63. Painter Spring: Mineral Specimens

Watch for this shed and group of trees when you get to Painter Spring.

**Land type:** High desert, mountains
**Elevation:** 5,328 feet
**GPS:** N39 11.287' / W113 26.656'
**Best seasons:** Spring and fall
**Land manager:** BLM
**Material:** Mineral specimens
**Tool:** Rock hammer
**Vehicle:** High-clearance
**Special attractions:** None
**Accommodations:** Motels; private camping and RV parking in Delta; plenty of camping areas at the site
**Finding the site:** From the viaduct on US 6 and US 50 at the west end of Delta, take US 6/50 west for 51.6 miles. You will see a sign to Painter Spring and a dirt

# Site 63

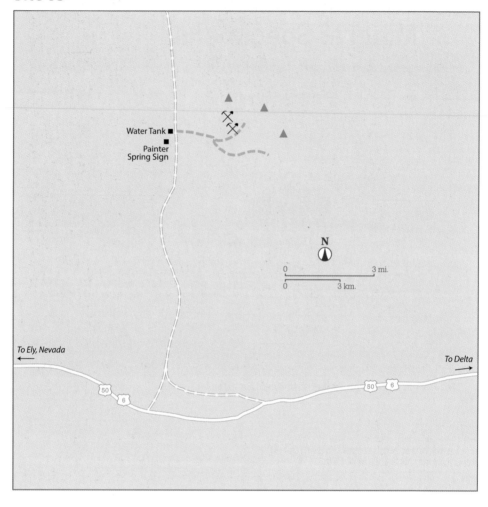

road going to the right. You may take this road or continue down the highway another 3.5 miles to another sign and road going right to Painter Spring. This second road is a little smoother, and you will have a little less dirt road to travel; otherwise it makes no difference. From the first turnoff it is 12.4 miles to the Painter Spring turnoff. The turnoff is well marked with a BLM sign. Follow the road toward the spring for about 1.5 miles; there is a wide spot to park. If you are a serious four-wheeler, you may want to drive a little farther. When we were there in 2012, this road was steep and narrow and you had to go to the very end of the

This road leads up to the spring.

road to turn around. It is best to just park and walk up to the spring; you will also find some good material along the way.

## Rockhounding

Painter Spring may not be at the end of the world, but if you stand on your tiptoes, you can see it. Some specimens, such as muscovite mica, pyrite, garnet, quartz, and pink feldspar, have been found here. Remember, this site is out on the loneliest road in America, so you will want to take plenty of water and combine this trip with the four other rockhounding sites—Conger Spring, Skull Rock Pass, Fossil Mountain, and Antelope Spring—in the area.

# 64. Fossil Mountain: Fossils

Fossils are still found in this area.

**Land type:** High desert
**Elevation:** 5,675 feet
**GPS:** N38 51.686' / W113 26.919'
**Best seasons:** Spring and fall
**Land manager:** BLM
**Material:** Fossils
**Tool:** Rock hammer
**Vehicle:** High-clearance
**Special attractions:** None
**Accommodations:** Motels; private camping and RV parking in Delta
**Finding the site:** From the top of the viaduct on US 6 and US 50 at the west end of Delta, go west on US 6/50 for 50.1 miles. Turn south onto a dirt road. At 0.9 mile you will come to a fork going right; keep straight ahead. At 2.2 miles you will come to another fork going left; keep to the right. At 4.2 miles you will see a road going

# Site 64

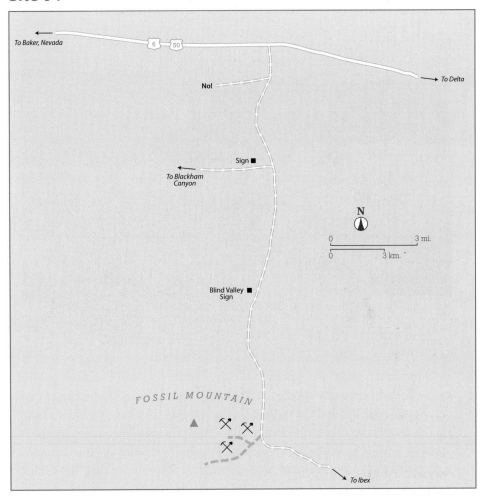

To Baker, Nevada

6  50

No!

To Delta

Sign ■

To Blackham
Canyon

N

0                3 mi.

0             3 km.

Blind Valley ■
Sign

FOSSIL MOUNTAIN

To Ibex

right to Blackham Canyon; keep straight ahead. At 8.1 miles a sign indicates you
are entering Blind Valley. At 14 miles you will come to a fork. The left fork goes to
Ibex. Take the right fork for 0.1 mile to a faint track to the right. Follow the track as
far as you can toward the mountain to the west. Park and hunt on both sides of
the road.

## Rockhounding

The material here is a conglomerate of many different fossils. Among them
are trilobites, brachiopods, and crinoids. They are of the Lower Ordovician

Walk up this road to the top of the hill, and there you'll find fossils.

epoch and are said to be found here in greater abundance and variety than in any other place in the western United States. More than thirteen fossil groups can be found at this one location. I found some nice pieces in the berms that the road grader had turned up, but I have a feeling the hunting would have been better closer to the mountain. At the time we were there, though, there was a large rock blocking the road. A serious four-wheeler could go around it (but not I). I also didn't feel like making the short hike to the mountain, since the July temperature was over 100°F, and I was afraid of becoming a fossil myself. Come out here in the fall and hike around; you will probably find some real keepers.

# 65. Antelope Spring: Trilobite Fossils

Gates have been placed across the road.

**Land type:** High desert
**Elevation:** 6,818 feet
**GPS:** N39 21.192' / W113 16.829'
**Best seasons:** Spring through fall
**Land manager:** BLM, private claims
**Material:** Trilobite fossils
**Tools:** Rock hammer, shale-splitting tool
**Vehicle:** Any
**Special attractions:** Little Sahara Recreation Area (see "Sights Along the Way")
**Accommodations:** Motels; private camping and RV parking in Delta; camping in and around the site
**Finding the site:** The accompanying map shows the general area of the trilobite beds, but the only sensible way to find them is to make inquiry in town. The beds

# Site 65

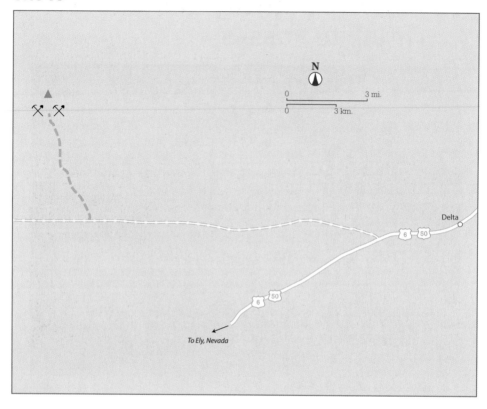

are under private claim, but it is possible to scratch around outside the boundaries of the claims and find some specimens. This is acceptable if you like to spend time wandering around the desert, but a quick trip to West Desert Collectors will get you where you want to go a lot easier. They hold some of the claims and give complete directions on how to get there, what to look for, and other information. They will give you written permission to collect on their claim. For information, contact West Desert Collectors, 278 West Main St., Delta, UT 84624; (801) 864-2175; fax: (801) 864-2180.

# 66. Sunstone Knoll: Labradorite

Stay just to the left of this mailbox, and travel to the top of the hill in the background.

**Land type:** High desert
**Elevation:** 4,584 feet
**GPS:** N39 8.939' / W112 43.125'
**Best seasons:** Spring and fall
**Land manager:** BLM, private claim
**Material:** Labradorite
**Tools:** Rock hammer, heavy hammers, chisels
**Vehicle:** Any
**Special attractions:** None
**Accommodations:** Motels; private RV parking in Delta
**Finding the site:** From the top of the viaduct at the west end of Delta on US 6 and US 50, go west for 4.3 miles to the intersection of UT 257. From the intersection, drive south on UT 257 for 13.4 miles. At this point a sign directs you to Sunstone Knoll. A dirt road to the left leads to a series of low hills just 0.5 mile

# Site 66

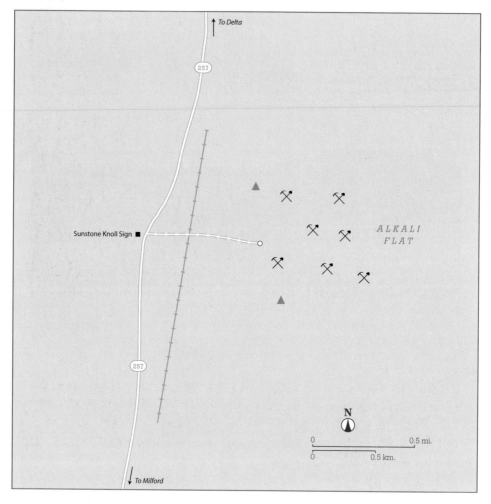

from the highway. As you leave the highway, you will cross the railroad tracks and come to a three-way fork. The middle fork has a mailbox with a sign stating that this is a private claim and requesting that you register on the log inside. Once registered, head up the middle fork to a turnaround and parking area. Actually there are a number of roads all over the area, but this is a good place to start your hunt. **Caution:** Be on the lookout for snakes; this is another area where they are thick.

A handful of sunstones (labradorite) found after just a 10-minute search

## Rockhounding

Labradorite is a variety of feldspar that contains sodium and calcium. The crystals found here are generally small, but there are bushels of them. Get the sun at your back, and the ground sparkles. The easiest way to collect is to go east of the hills to the large alkali flat and just pick crystals up off the ground. Most will be from ⅛ to ¼ inch, and the ones on top of the ground will be clear. To get the real gems, you will have to go up on the hills and attack the boulders with a vengeance. It is hard work, and there are no guarantees, but if you look at some of the broken rock below, you will see the types of treasures that await you. Maybe you will find a pocket with the mother of all labradorite in it. On the other hand, maybe you will hit your thumb with your hammer and lose your hat.

# 67. Black Rock 1: Obsidian

Look down as you get out of your car or truck. The better stuff is up the hill.

**Land type:** High desert
**Elevation:** 4,578 feet
**GPS:** N38 49.245' / W112 48.906'
**Best seasons:** Spring and fall
**Land manager:** BLM
**Materials:** Black, snowflake, and mahogany obsidian
**Tool:** Rock hammer
**Vehicle:** Any
**Special attractions:** None
**Accommodations:** Motels; private RV parking in Delta
**Finding the site:** From the top of the viaduct on US 6 and US 50 at the west end of Delta, go west for 4.3 miles to the intersection with UT 257. Drive south from the intersection on UT 257 for 36.4 miles. At this point a gravel road goes left.

# Site 67

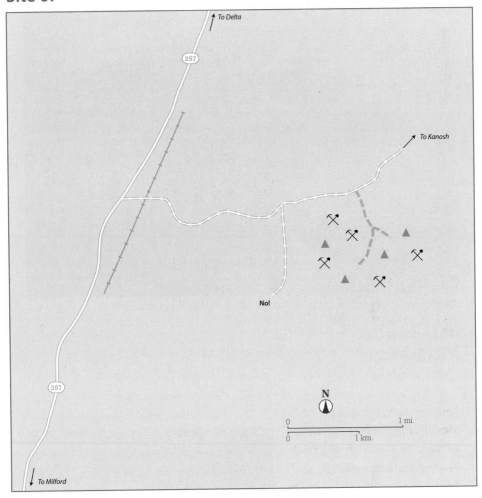

There is a sign stating that the road goes to Kanosh, but the last time we were there, the sign on the southbound side of the highway was missing. Keep a sharp eye on the odometer. When you get on the road to Kanosh, follow it for 2.3 miles to a rather faint track going right. Just before you reach the indicated mileage, some tracks go up a hill to your right. Don't be fooled. Just around the bend are the ones you want, and they don't go uphill. Follow the tracks for 0.3 mile to a fork. Park anywhere, and search all the hills and washes.

You need to do some looking but snowflake obsidian can still be found at this site.

## Rockhounding

There is beautiful black obsidian all over this area, and a little searching will turn up some nice specimens of snowflake and mahogany obsidian. The gravel road is literally paved with small black pieces. As usual, to find big pieces you will have to do some walking and maybe a little digging, but the work will be worth it.

Be on the lookout for nice pieces of mahogany obsidian in this area.

# 68. Black Rock 2: Obsidian

Look for this road, which is 2.2 miles from the main road and the sign that says TO KANOSH 26 MILES.

**Land type:** Cedar-covered hills
**Elevation:** 4,856 feet
**GPS:** N38 45.872' / W112 53.449'
**Best seasons:** Spring and fall
**Land manager:** BLM
**Material:** Obsidian
**Tool:** Rock hammer
**Vehicle:** Any
**Special attractions:** None
**Accommodations:** Motels; private camping and RV parking in Delta
**Finding the site:** From the top of the viaduct on US 6 and US 50 at the west end of Delta, go west for 4.3 miles to the

Obsidian is lying all over the ground in this productive area.

# Site 68

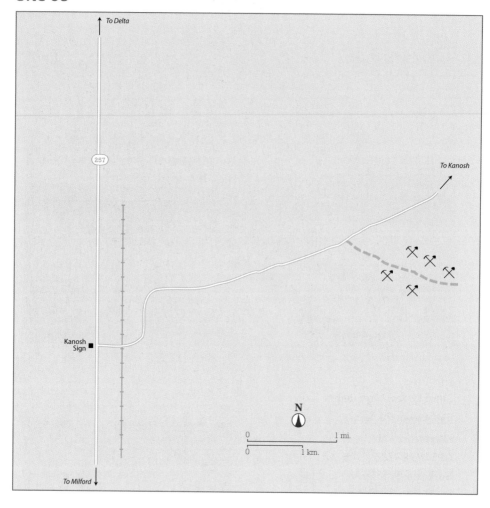

intersection with UT 257. Drive south from the intersection on UT 257 for 42.4 miles. At this point a dirt road goes left. A sign states that Kanosh is 26 miles. Follow this road for 2.2 miles, where another dirt road goes right. Take this road for 0.3 mile and park.

## Rockhounding

This is a good site for picking up some nice obsidian while expending virtually no effort. The little hills in the cedars are covered with it. Most are black, but there are pieces of snowflake and a little mahogany. Take a lunch, and spend some time. You will take home a nice assortment.

# 69. Milford: Obsidian

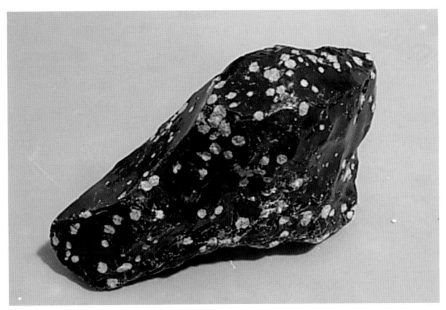

Snowflake obsidian, Milford, Utah

**Land types:** High desert, hills
**Elevation:** 6,382 feet
**GPS:** N38 29.310' / W112 50.046'
**Best seasons:** Spring and fall
**Land manager:** BLM
**Material:** Obsidian
**Tool:** Rock hammer
**Vehicle:** Any
**Special attractions:** None
**Accommodations:** Motels; public and private RV parking and camping in Beaver
**Finding the site:** From the top of the viaduct on US 6 and US 50 at the west end of Delta, go west for 4.3 miles to the intersection with UT 257. Drive south from the intersection on UT 257 to Milford. The mileage from the center of Milford on UT 257 to the road to the geothermal plant is 4.2 miles north. Continue past the plant for about 0.5 mile. At this point the road will fork. Take the right fork and continue for about 0.2 mile. Actually, the distance is not critical, since you will be driving

# Site 69

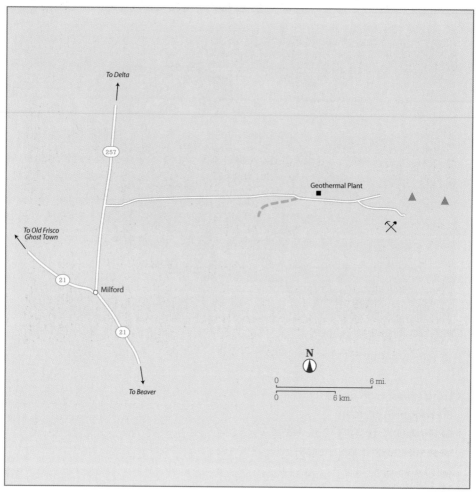

To Delta

257

Geothermal Plant

To Old Frisco
Ghost Town

21

Milford

21

To Beaver

N

0                   6 mi.
0                6 km.

over obsidian all the way. At 0.7 mile, however, there is a very rough bulldozer road going up the hill to your left. This rut is solid obsidian. Park and enjoy.

## Rockhounding

The majority of the obsidian here is the banded black variety, but we also found sheen and swirl, as well as a little snowflake and mahogany. There is so much nice cutting material here that in order to take home as much as you would like, you will have to leave the picnic cooler, the spare tire, the diaper bags, and maybe one or two of the kids behind.

# 70. Minersville: Mineral Specimens

This road takes you into the mine tailings of Minersville.

**Land type:** Mountains
**Elevation:** 5,284 feet
**GPS:** N38 15.738' / W112 15.905'
**Best seasons:** Spring through fall
**Land manager:** BLM
**Material:** Mineral specimens
**Tool:** Rock hammer
**Vehicle:** High-clearance recommended
**Special attractions:** None
**Accommodations:** Motels; public and private camping and RV parking in the Beaver, Milford, and Minersville areas
**Finding the site:** From the railroad tracks at the south end of Milford, drive south on UT 21 toward Minersville to mile marker 89. If you are coming from the Minersville area, just look for the same mile marker. A dirt road just north of this

# Site 70

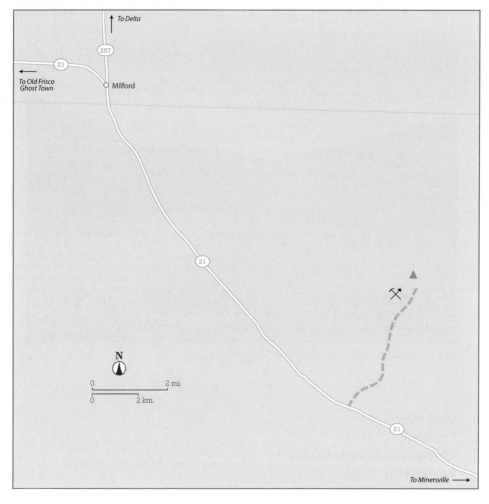

mile marker goes left toward the hills. Follow this road for 3 miles to the first of several mine tailings piles. We stopped here for the GPS reading, and there are a number of roads going from this point to various mine diggings. Where we stopped was at the old mine loading site.

## Rockhounding

Explore all the tailings along the road for such specimens as pyrite, bornite, galena, quartz, and fluorite. You may not find them all, but they are there. Be prepared to do a little searching.

# 71. Beaver: Agate

If you walk this road to the top, you're likely to find some agates.

**Land type:** Hills
**Elevation:** 6,224 feet
**GPS:** N38 13.946' / W112 37.071'
**Best seasons:** Spring through fall
**Land manager:** BLM
**Material:** Agate
**Tool:** Rock hammer
**Vehicle:** Any (high-clearance or four-wheel-drive to some areas)
**Special attractions:** None
**Accommodations:** Motels; public and private RV parking and camping in the Beaver area
**Finding the site:** We had a lot of fun finding this site. It is in an old collecting area, and I had been carrying around information on how to get there for years. Even though we had been through Beaver many times, we had never had the time to

# Site 71

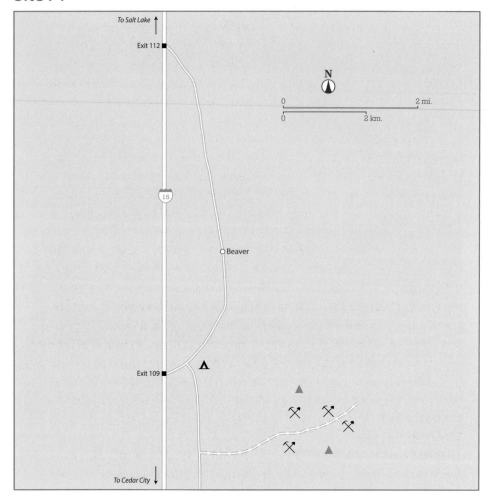

To Salt Lake

Exit 112

N

0                       2 mi.

0                 2 km.

15

Beaver

Exit 109

To Cedar City

stop and hunt. This time we were really looking forward to a good time. So much for looking forward.

We went to the spot where we supposedly turn onto the gravel road, but there was no gravel road. We cruised the frontage road several times, but nothing seemed right. The road we thought we wanted went down a little hill and into an irrigated field. Determined to find the site, we returned to the big campground to ask directions. It was closed, but a gentleman who professed to be a former rockhound gave us his version of directions. They put us in a spot where there was not a semblance of a road anywhere.

I decided to check at a forest service office near Beaver. My information called it Blue Valley, but Blue Valley was a good 10 miles from where we had been looking. Several forest service personnel had no idea where the site might be, despite some map checking. Finally we got directions to South Creek Road, mentioned in the information we had. About 9 miles later we decided this wasn't it either. Back to Beaver for one more try.

Even the rock shop in Beaver was closed. (Was this the *Twilight Zone*?) As we turned around in the shop yard, the owner showed up, and I told him our tale of woe. Finally, someone who knew what we were looking for! I got pinpoint directions, down to the bales of hay on each side of the road. The correct road turned out to be the one leading to the irrigated field. We were told to follow it toward the hills.

Off we went, with our spirit of adventure rekindled. Down the hill we sailed onto the road across the field. There was just one minor problem: The field was being irrigated with those industrial-strength mega sprinklers, and they were right next to the road. The road itself was a muddy canal. No problem. I just put the old horse into four-wheel drive, low, and drove on, slipping and sliding along and getting splattered with water. At this point the road turned right and headed across another field—a dry one. At the other end we came to a nice graded gravel road that—you guessed it—ran from the frontage road we had been on to the hills we were headed for. Some days are like that! I promise that if you adhere to the following directions, you will have a pleasant trip—and won't get your vehicle washed in the process.

The main street in Beaver is actually a business loop that runs between I-15 exit 109 on the south to exit 112 on the north. At the south end of the loop, a frontage road continues south past a large campground. From the intersection, drive 1.3 miles south to a good gravel road going left. Follow this road for 1.6 miles. Keep an eye out for a large pole line with orange balls on the wires. At the 1.6-mile mark, a pole line road goes up the hill to the right; you will be directly under the orange balls. The pole line road is rough, but four-wheelers can make it. If you do not have four-wheel drive, park off the road and walk up the hill. It is a short hike, and there is material to be found along the way that you wouldn't see from a bouncing vehicle.

There is good hunting all over the tops of the hills and in the washes. There is a lot of country out here, so allow plenty of time for exploration if you can. On the north side of the gravel road, you can see the area I had been looking for. It is now on private land, and the owner has closed it to collecting. There are other areas of private land out here, so be sure you don't trespass.

## Rockhounding

The material that was so sought after in years past was a beautiful blue agate called Blue Valley agate, or just Beaver blue agate. In looking around at this site, I could not come up with very much agate. I admit that I did not search much or go far from the road, so you might want to take the time to walk and look a bit farther afield.

# TOOLS OF THE TRADE

As you go out on these excursions, there is one thing in common that everyone should have in their possession: tools to extract your treasures with. As I have been out rock hunting for many years, I have put together a bag of tools that I always pack with me where ever I go. The first and most important tool is a good rock hammer. These come in a variety of sizes and weights, so don't just settle for the first one that you see. Look around and chose a good one that fits your needs. Make sure that the weight of the hammer is right for you, and it has a comfortable handle, as you are going to be using this a lot in just about every place you go in Utah.

Next item will be a chisel. These also come in a variety of sizes. I have two that I take with me. One has a pointed tip and one has a flat tip, so depending on the situation, I have something to loosen the rocks. I have a pack of small screw drivers that I use to check out cracks and fissures that may have small hidden gems in them. One with a nice long shank is especially helpful. These are also used for picking out smaller pieces of rocks. Make sure that you have a bag to place your findings in, and things that you can wrap around your treasures to keep them from breaking. Take paper towels, tissues, or small baggies to help keep your treasures safe. If you are out where you are going after small gems, a pill bottle or two helps keeps your gems from being lost or broken in your bag.

These items can be thrown into a backpack or small bag and should only weigh around 10 pounds. This way you can pack more out with you. If you are going on some hard digging, you will need to have a good shovel and pick and also a breaker bar to help get your rocks out of the ground. Remember, when you dig a hole, be sure and cover it back up when you leave. These are just a few basic tools that I have and where I am going, or what I am going after, will determine what I pack, but these I usually have with me all the time. As you get out and start rockhounding in earnest, you will find tools that will suit your needs and can add them to your pack, but remember that you do not want to over fill your pack, so that you cannot carry out your finds with you. One of the places where I get my tools is a small company called Geo-tools, and the owner has been into rock hunting for many years and knows what tools work best. Look it up on Geo-tools.com. I have a Wizard Wreaking Bar and the Eastwing Paleo Pick from them and they are great basic tools for the rock hunter.

A must to always carry with you is plenty of water, snacks, sunscreen, and a small first aid kit. Make sure someone always knows where you are going because safety is the number one concern!

# GLOSSARY

**Agate:** A form of chalcedony containing bands or mossy inclusions. Often very colorful, but sometimes with either one color or very muted colors.

**Aggregate:** A mixture of different kinds of rocks or crystals.

**Alabaster:** A fine-grained variety of gypsum used widely for carving.

**Amethyst:** A gemstone of the quartz family ranging in color from pale lilac to deep purple.

**Ammonite:** A cephalopod fossil curled like a ram's horn.

**Aquamarine:** A form of beryl next in desirability to emerald. Colors range from pale to deep blue or blue green.

**Azurite:** A blue copper carbonate often associated with malachite.

**Barite:** Barium sulfate occurring in blue, green, brown, and red colors.

**Beryl:** Beryllium aluminum sulfate, which is colorless in its pure form. Colored varieties include emerald, green; aquamarine, blue; morganite, pink; and heliodor, brown to golden yellow.

**Biotite:** A member of the mica group usually in black, brown-black, or green-black.

**Book:** Term for a common occurrence of mica in leaves that resemble the pages of a book.

**Cabbing:** The act of creating a cabochon.

**Cabochon (cab):** A common shape for a gem, usually with an elliptical perimeter and a domed top.

**Calcite:** Calcium carbonate that occurs in clear crystals as well as white, brown, red, yellow, and blue.

**Cephalopod:** Free-swimming marine animal. Ammonites and baculites are typical of cephalopods.

**Chalcedony:** A cryptocrystalline form of quartz in which the crystal structure is not visible to the naked eye. The forms include agate, jasper, carnelian, sard, onyx, chrysoprase, sardonyx, and flint.

**Chalcedony rose:** A chalcedony formation resembling a rose.

**Chrysocolla:** A cyan (blue-green) color and is a minor ore of copper, having a hardness of 2.5 to 7.0. It is of secondary origin and forms in the oxidation zones of copper ore bodies. Associated minerals are quartz, limonite, azurite, malachite, cuprite, and other secondary copper minerals.

**Concretion:** A cemented accumulation of mineral material. Common concretions may contain pyrite, silica, calcite, or gypsum.

**Coprolite:** Fossilized excrement in sedimentary rock.

**Country rock:** The common rock surrounding a vein or other deposit of gemstones or minerals.

**Crinoid:** One of hundreds of round stem-like echinoderms. Usually only parts are found as fossils.

**Crystal:** A solid mineral having a regular geometric shape with flat faces or surfaces.

**Dendrite:** A mineral inclusion in a rock that resembles the branching of a fern.

**Dike:** A wall of igneous rock surrounded by country rock.

**Epidote:** Green crystal sometimes used as a gemstone, but more commonly collected for display.

**Feldspar:** The most abundant minerals in the Earth's crust. Feldspars are classified as orthoclase and plagioclase. Among the most desired varieties are moonstone, sunstone, microcline, and labradorite.

**Float:** Gemstones, minerals, and other materials that have been transported from their place of origin by water, erosion, or gravity.

**Fluorite:** A common mineral that occurs in white, brown, purple, green, yellow, violet, and blue. Although it is sometimes faceted, it is too soft to stand up to the day-to-day wear of jewelry.

**Fluorspar:** A less pure and more granular form of fluorite.

**Fortification agate:** Agate with acutely banded corners that form a closed figure resembling a fort.

**Fossils:** Remains of plants, insects, or animals preserved in either casts or molds.

**Gangue:** Country rock or other rock of no value surrounding minerals or gemstones.

**Garnet:** A group of differently colored but chemically similar minerals. The group includes pyrope, red with brown; almandine, red with violet; spessartite, orange to red brown; grossular, yellow to copper brown; demantoid, emerald green; and uvarovite, emerald green.

**Gem:** A gemstone that has been prepared for use in jewelry.

**Gemstone:** Any precious or semi-precious stone that can be cut and/or polished for jewelry.

**Geode:** A hollow nodule or concretion, usually filled with crystal formations.

**Gypsum:** A hydrous calcium sulfate that occurs in white, gray, brown, red, and yellow. There is also a colorless variety called selenite, and the dense form is called alabaster.

**Igneous:** One of the three primary classifications of rock formed by solidification or crystallization of magma.

**Jasper:** Opaque form of chalcedony, often with mossy inclusions or intertwining of various colors.

**Lapidary:** The art of forming and shaping gemstones or one who does so.

**Lepidolite:** Pink- to lilac-colored silicate mineral of the mica group.

**Limonite:** A term applied generally to a brownish iron hydroxide. Often occurs as a pseudomorph after iron minerals such as pyrite.

**Malachite:** A green copper ore that occurs both in crystal and massive forms. The massive forms are often banded and many contain beautiful bull's-eyes.

**Massive form:** The form of a mineral in which the crystals are either very small or without any discernible definition.

**Matrix:** Material in which a mineral crystal or fossil is embedded.

**Metamorphic:** Pre-existing rock changed by the action of pressure, chemical action, or heat. One of the three primary classifications of rock.

**Mica:** A group of sheet silicate minerals whose major members are muscovite, biotite, phlogopite, lepidolite, and chlorite.

**Micromount:** A tiny mineral specimen intended for viewing under a microscope.

**Muscovite:** One of the mica group. Usually colorless to pale yellow, green, pink, or brown.

**Onyx:** A black-and-white-banded chalcedony. The colored varieties sold in gift shops are either dyed onyx or a form of calcite or aragonite.

**Opal:** A silicon oxide closely related to chalcedony, but softer and containing water. Common opal is often dull and not suitable for jewelry, but some have a waxy texture and will cut and polish into nice cabochons. Common opal often replaces wood fibers in fossil wood and makes finely detailed samples. Precious opal is the type associated with fine jewelry and shows beautiful flashes of multicolored fire. It is often mistakenly called fire opal, but true fire opal is red and does not have the flashes of fire.

**Ozokerite:** A hard mineral wax once used widely for everything from water-proofing of matches to making statues for wedding cakes.

**Pegmatite:** Coarse-grained igneous rock often the host for gemstones and minerals. Usually found as smaller masses in large igneous formations.

**Pelecypods:** Bi-valved mollusks with shells that meet evenly at the hinge. The shells are not symmetrical as in the brachiopods. Oysters, clams, and mussels are typical pelecypods.

**Petrification:** The process by which silica or other minerals replace the cell structure of organic material.

**Porphry:** Rock containing crystals in a fine-grained mass.

**Pseudomorph:** A crystal with the geometric appearance of one mineral, but which has been chemically replaced with another mineral.

**Pyrite:** Iron sulfide or disulfide with a brassy yellow color. Commonly called fool's gold.

**Quartz:** Silicon dioxide, white, colorless, and in various shades including amethyst, aventurine, citrine, rose quartz, smoky quartz, and tiger eye.

**Rhodochrosite:** A manganese carbonate gemstone in colors from rose red to white with striping. Sometimes forms as stalactites in caves.

**Rhodonite:** A deep red to pink gemstone usually with black manganese oxide inclusions that often appear as spider webbing.

**Rhyolite:** An extrusive igneous rock, primarily composed of quartz and feldspar.

**Sedimentary:** Rock formed by deposition, compaction, and cementation. One of the three primary classifications of rock.

**Septarian nodule:** A spherical concretion with an internal polygonal system of calcite-filled cracks.

**Silicified:** A mineral or organic compound that has been replaced by silica.

**Syringapora:** An extinct genus of phaceloid tabulate coral. It has been found in rocks ranging in age from the Ordovician to the Permian, although it was most widespread during the Silurian, Devonian, and Carboniferous periods. Among other places, it has been found in the Columbus Limestone in Ohio, and in the Spring Branch Member of the Lecompton Limestone in Kansas.

**Tailings:** Waste material from mining or milling.

# SITE INDEX

# About the Authors

**William A. Kappele** has been rockhounding across the West for more than forty years. His other books include *Rockhounding Nevada* and *Rockhounding Colorado*.

**Gary Warren** was born and raised in Clearfield, Utah. He and his wife eventually settled in Brigham City, Utah. They have four children, fifteen grandchildren, and three great-grandchildren. Gary has been a member of the Cache Rock and Gem Club, located in Logan, Utah, for ten years, eight of which he served as president. He enjoys sharing his love of rockhounding with children through school lectures and after-school group demonstrations and activities. The club has also incorporated a Junior Rockhounding program. Recently retired, Gary has more time to pursue his passions, traveling and rockhounding throughout Utah.